£1

UNDERGROUND IN JAPAN

UNDERGROUND IN JAPAN

Rey Ventura

*Edited and Introduced by James Fenton
with an Afterword by Ian Buruma*

JONATHAN CAPE
LONDON

First published 1992
© Reynald B. Ventura 1992
Jonathan Cape, 20 Vauxhall Bridge Road, London SW1V 2SA

Reynald B. Ventura has asserted his right under the Copyright,
Designs and Patents Act 1988 to be identified as the
author of this work

A CIP catalogue record for this book is available from the
British Library

ISBN 0-224-03550-9

Printed in Great Britain by
St Edmundsbury Press, Bury St Edmunds, Suffolk

Contents

	Introduction by James Fenton	vii
1	Independence	3
2	Adopted Son	10
3	The Welcoming Party	17
4	A Standing Man	25
5	The Queen of Koto	33
6	How Arguments Begin	39
7	Juan, Margie, Miguel	46
8	Kotobuki Sketchbook	55
9	In and Out of the Underground	64
10	Filipino Sunday	74
11	The Missionary	91
12	Scissors, Paper, Stone	105
13	A Stabbing	114
14	Love, Death, Etcetera	127
15	Zaldy's Advice	140
16	Sumimasen, Gommennasai	149
17	The Second America	156

18 I Surrender   168
    Japalog Dictionary   174
    Afterword by Ian Buruma   185

Introduction

WE DO NOT often find descriptions of pioneer immigrant societies in the making, for the simple reason that the people involved in them are too busy, too tired by the end of the day, too close to the struggle to be able to see it as a subject. Nor is the illegal immigrant very likely to want to publicise his activities, or to open up his world to the visiting writer. His secrets are his stock in trade, after all.

But the thought of the great migrant societies at the moment of their birth is immensely fascinating. What wouldn't we give for a slave's journal, an Italian set of letters home from New York, anything that gave a feeling for the texture of life as it was *then* ... Epics have been written, novels and films inspired by such a sense of 'then'. The purpose of this book is to look at such a world as it is now, the world of the illegal worker in Japan.

Long famous for being an enclosed, exclusive society, Japan is now – like it or not – a target of immigration. In 1989, for the first time, the number of foreigners deported for violation of immigration laws exceeded 20,000, and that figure was up more than 25 per cent on the year before. Most of the deportees came from the labour underground, most of them were male, and the largest single group was Filipino, with Pakistanis and Koreans coming a close second and third.

By how much should one multiply this number of deportees to arrive at the actual number of illegal workers in Japan? The Ministry of Justice estimated for that year (the year in which the author of this book was deported) there were 100,000 illegal foreigners, but a more recent unofficial figure suggests something nearer a quarter of a million. At all events enough to people a considerable city.

Or, more accurately, not one secret city but several mutually exclusive secret societies, peopled by Filipinos, Pakistanis, Koreans, Bangladeshis, Malaysians, Thais and, the smallest of the main groups, Chinese. Most of the men work in construction or in factories, most of the women as hostesses in bars. Their employers, it would seem, need them, but absolutely no provision is made for their work to be legally acknowledged.

The process of dropping out into such a labour underground has been well-known for years in the

Philippines, where it is called T.N.T. – *tago-ng-tago* or 'always hiding'. It is a technique widely practised in the infiltration of the United States. But the idea of going T.N.T. in Japan is relatively new, and dates roughly from the time of the rise of the yen. As the author of this book observes, the rewards are such as to have made Japan replace the States in the Filipino imagination as the Eldorado of the future.

It is, of course, only one of several major countries to which Filipinos travel in search of work, legal or otherwise, in pursuit of which they are prepared to undergo all kinds of privations. It was not until reading the journals which Rey Ventura kept during his time in Japan that I learnt the answer to something that had often puzzled me. Those who have been migrant workers, in Saudi Arabia for instance, are not slow to tell you how dreadful life can be, of the disruptive effect on the family, of the sacrifices and homesickness involved. And yet on several striking occasions I have come across people who will give up a reasonably well-paid job in order to work abroad. In one case, the man had already had his marriage break up during a stint in Saudi. Now he was planning to go back. When he told me what he was expecting to earn it was only a marginal improvement on what I was paying him, and that margin would be wiped out by the expenses he would incur. By the standards of the barrio he had a very cushy job. Why would he throw that in?

Rey's observation that it was not the homeless and unemployed of the Philippines who sought work abroad, but precisely the people who already had some marginal advantage in the economy, seemed to me quite fresh. Migrate is what you do *when the opportunity arises*, not what you do for lack of opportunity. Starting from that perception, one can begin to understand the migrant worker. Pessimism about the homeland definitely comes into it (my employee wanted to go to Saudi because he had more faith in the Saudi economy than in my ability to make a success of a fish farm – and not without some reason) but there is a positive side to the deal.

From the point of view of the host country, the migrant worker may be the lowest of the low. From the point of view of those back home he may be much envied and admired: he has won status in the barrio for himself and for his family. The world he creates around himself may mirror the world back home – with its religiosity, its clannishness and its networks – or it may constitute a brilliant escape from taboo. Family life is abandoned in favour of polygamy, poly-andry, a sort of bohemianism in which father and son can live together by a completely different set of rules from those which they would observe back home. When a man migrates in search of work, his real aims may be quite different from his stated aims: he may think he is out to earn a certain amount of money when in fact he is after status. The travel alone – the first trip across the ocean – will earn him merit.

The world of Kotobuki, the Filipino enclave in Yokohama described here, is sordid in all its externals. And yet it is possible for its inhabitants to say, 'Koto is paradise.' What could be meant by such an expression is part of the subject of this book – for all its deprivations, the migrant worker's life has its seductive side, its own lure. A refined morality does not last long in Koto, but the somewhat battered outlook which does survive deserves, I think, such respect as it gets here. This is a book about ordinary life conducted under the extraordinary conditions of exile and secrecy.

JAMES FENTON

UNDERGROUND IN JAPAN

I

Independence

I WOKE AT four in the morning, as agreed, and lay there, stretching my feet towards the *kotatsu* heater. Akihiro didn't move. Each time a car passed, the wooden lodging-house shook slightly. I was paralysed, too shy to reach and wake Akihiro, and aware too that the landlord mustn't know that he had guests. The walls were made of plywood and asbestos. There was a sound of dripping. I watched the tiny luminous dial on the table and at four-thirty I knew we had missed the first Yokohama train. An hour passed. By now it was too late to find a job.

This had been going on for three days. All the time we talked about getting a job, but Akihiro was what he called 'a rare kind' of Japanese. He was lazy. Between his journalistic work he lived on *arbeito* – construction work, dish-washing, handing out fliers. He lived on cigarettes, black coffee and noodles. He only worked hard when the rent was overdue or the telephone about to be cut off. I was dependent on him to show me where to find a job. Until that happened, I was dependent on him for everything.

The room was bitter. I couldn't put the bedding over my head because of the smell. My bladder was full, but I couldn't get to the door without waking Kazuo, who slept at right-angles to us, sharing the kotatsu. One night I solved this problem by pissing out of the window, but this itself was an elaborate operation, with a great danger of embarrassment and scandal.

Now there was a sound of grinding teeth. Maybe that was Kazuo. He had just made a lot of money on an assignment, and I was waiting for him to lend me some of it. Kazuo usually seemed to be in work – he had come to photojournalism without formal train-ing, learning the technique of lighting, for instance, in the studio of a soft-porn magazine. He was on the way to success as a news photographer, but at this stage he couldn't afford a room in Tokyo. I'd been living off his kindness for too long.

At ten o'clock I got up and gently slid open the door. Kazuo moved his head away. As I was brushing my teeth at the sink in the corridor, I looked up to see that the blinding white roofs were covered in snow. It was early spring and I wanted to go to the park, but I was afraid that if I left the house unaccompanied the landlord would think I was a thief.

Akihiro's room smelt of cigarettes, bedding and

socks. Magazines and newspapers were piled up beside the tatami, and his books gathered dust. The table was scattered with old coffee filters and there was no ventilation. Akihiro lay in bed smoking the first stick of the day. As soon as Kazuo woke, they would resume their endless conversations.

They had great plans for an article on Filipino migrant workers around the world. Akihiro would write it. Kazuo would take the photographs. They would go wherever we had gone – to Saudi, to Europe, South-East Asia, even America. They could spend all day discussing this, with only coffee in their stomachs. I wanted to be included, at least in the planning stage, but this was not to be. I could only catch the drift of their conversation.

And then Akihiro could spend hours talking Filipino politics. He knew more than I did, but his knowledge was specialised. He could tell you everything about the Filipinos who collaborated during the Japanese occupation. To me, naturally, these people were traitors, but to Akihiro they were enlightened. He would offer to show me the grave of one of them who had died in Japan. He believed that if only the Japanese had got to the Philippines before the Americans things would have been very different. We would have been a better sort of colony.

Old smoke, old socks and the Great East Asia Co-Prosperity Sphere. Akihiro had not yet told me of the other great plan forming in his mind, which was to go wherever the Japanese had gone on their imperial adventure, although the history of that period was already an obsession with him. At one point, he took a job on a liberal paper whose politics he despised, simply in order to have access to their cuttings library. Korea, Taiwan, the Philippines – these were lost possessions to him.

At heart, although they were careful not to say it in so many words, Kazuo and Akihiro regretted the fact that the Emperor was no longer treated as a divinity. It was MacArthur's fault, they said. Once, when I made a comparison between Hirohito and Marcos, they flared up. Marcos is nothing, they said, pointing to the tips of their little fingers to show what they meant. To compare the dying Emperor in Tokyo with the dying dictator in Hawaii was sacrilege, but beyond rising to my taunt on this occasion they would never trust me enough to reveal their true feelings about the Emperor, the War and the destiny of Japan. I could deduce much from the way, for instance, the American-imposed constitution still rankled with them and the delight with which they compared Japan favourably with the States. The Japanese passport was the number one passport in the world, the yen the most powerful currency, and we had reached the stage where GI wives around the bases were selling their bodies to Japanese salarymen!

Kazuo and Akihiro were kind to me, but I was keen to get away from them. Kazuo couldn't show his face in Kotobuki, where the Filipinos lived; he had recently published photographs of illegal migrant workers, and the community objected. I was penniless, and I couldn't wait around until Akihiro decided to wake up early and get a job. Also, I was afraid I wouldn't survive much longer on black coffee and noodles.

At two in the afternoon, I reached for my bag, stood up and said, 'I'm going.' They were shocked. Was I going by myself? Yes, I said. Did I know the place? I said maybe I could still remember it.

Then Kazuo said, 'Leave your passport and blue card here, and any other ID.'

I knew Kazuo was going to say this. He seemed to want to keep me at his mercy. My passport contained a visa valid for one month; I'd got my blue card as a student and I was not yet doing anything illegal. If the police stopped me I could prove all that. But Kazuo said that the Filipinos I was going to work with were all illegal immigrants. If they knew of my student status, they would not accept me into their group. If the police saw my blue card, they might question my former school and create difficulties for them.

But there was something else behind Kazuo's reasoning. He had brought me back to Japan and had paid for everything so far. I was part of a story he was working on. I was one of his subjects. If I was arrested, I was supposed to contact him. Then he would come to the police station, rescue me – and take my photo. Behind bars would look good.

Now it was one thing to provide Kazuo with a convenient episode for a photo essay, quite another to go down to Yokohama with no papers in my pocket. Supposing there was an accident at work – how would they identify me? I didn't want to die anonymously. I didn't want simply to disappear after working in some chemical plant, as one Filipino had, a few months earlier.

Without a word, I put the papers in the pocket of my denim jacket and buttoned the flap. Kazuo grew agitated. 'Believe me, Rey,' he said. 'I'm a professional.' Always, when he got angry, he would claim to be a professional. 'I'm Japanese and we are in Japan.'

I was too angry to answer. Kazuo turned to Akihiro and asked him, in Japanese, to plead with me. Then he went on, in English, 'My friend Rey, your logic is wrong. You believe one plus one equals three.'

'I'm sorry,' I said. 'I don't believe in logic.'

Kazuo muttered under his breath. Now he was mad at me, and I had to ask him for that loan. I swallowed my pride. 'How much?' said Kazuo. Ten thousand yen would do. He took the note from an envelope and handed it to me brusquely.

When I bid the two of them goodbye, Kazuo didn't say a word.

I tiptoed downstairs, opened the front door without a sound and gently manoeuvred the gate that led to the street. At first it felt great, to have space, to be able to breathe, to be alone. After the imprisonment of the last few days, it was as if a new life was beginning. The snow had disappeared from the street, but it still lay on the rooftops under the overcast sky. It was cold and I felt hungry.

But as I waited for my order in the noodle shop everything suddenly changed. My appetite went. I felt drained. I felt angry with myself for not having argued properly with Kazuo. I had been so helpless, waiting around, being treated like a child, feeling like a parasite.

But now that I had made my bid for independence, I recalled that I did *not* really know where I was going. I had no address with me. I knew that I must take the blue train to Yokohama, but I couldn't recall how to get from there to Kotobuki.

I stared down at my noodles as the tears began to come. I thought of going home, but I didn't have a plane ticket. The money I had borrowed might last me two days. I was on my way to a dangerous Yokohama slum, in the hope of finding work which would probably also be dangerous. And if I succeeded in finding work I would automatically have to go underground. I would have to become invisible, like tens of thousands of Filipinos who live by the system we call T.N.T. – *tago-ng-tago*, 'always in hiding'.

2

Adopted Son

AFTER YOKOHAMA STATION, you begin to get glimpses of the docks and patches of sea behind the new construction sites. I watched the helmeted workers laying foundations, and imagined myself in that kind of job. All the time, I was trying to remember the characters for the station I wanted. Was it River-Mountain, or Mountain-River, or River-Stone? In between stations a voice would announce the next stop, but I wouldn't be certain which was the right one until I saw the characters themselves.

We passed through Sukuragicho and Kannai – monotonous, indifferentiated stretches of office blocks with no space to breathe. I was scanning the faces of fellow passengers in the hope of finding a Filipino, but it was working hours and there were still no foreigners around. I kept wondering where I would spend the night. Then the voice on the intercom said, '*Ishikawa-eki desu,*

Ishikawa-eki desu.' The characters were Stone-River. I got out.

And now I just walked, without the least idea where I was going, following the crowd past the pachinko parlours, the love hotels and the electronic shops. It was drizzling. Still guided only by instinct, I reached an intersection in the road. In one direction, there were tall offices. In the other, the street grew deserted and the buildings ugly – grey, unpainted concrete apartments thrown together with no concession to design and giving no sign of life at all. And still no Filipino face.

At the end of this depressing street stood a solitary building which, although it had no particular distinguishing features, suddenly seemed familiar, and I knew that if I got inside it I would recognise the lay-out. Kazuo had taken me here the previous year, when I was a student, and had got me to pose in a room. The photograph had appeared in a Japanese magazine as a portrait of an illegal worker. If you looked closely, however, you would have seen that I was wearing a Pierre Cardin hand-me-down from my brother. Kazuo had lived in this building until the time his pictures were published, and the real workers he had photographed were outraged.

I could remember three names. There was Rogelio, whose girlfriend had told me he would help me, and there was Jojo and his Japanese live-in partner, Yuri.

I tried to look casual as I entered the building.

The lay-out was as I expected, with the *papa-san*'s desk just by the door. I explained to him that I was just visiting Jojo and Yuri. He nodded without much interest and let me pass.

The building seemed to have been designed for dwarves, with ceilings on the staircase so low you had to duck. I groped along a narrow corridor, listening at the doorways for the sound of a Filipino voice, and feeling like a spy. Outside the last room I heard a woman giggling, followed by a man's voice speaking in broken Japanese.

I knocked. '*Dare desu ka?*' said the man. 'Who's there?'

'*Pilipino ako?*' I said. 'I'm a Filipino.'

After a moment, the woman who had giggled opened the door and I was astonished. She turned out to be the size of a sumo wrestler. She blocked my way, leaving the Filipino with the option of climbing out of the window should I chance to be an immigration agent.

As I asked for the number of Jojo and Yuri's room, the sumo wrestler kept her hand firmly on the doorknob, while the man sat tensed as if ready to spring. The room turned out to be just opposite.

Yuri opened the door, pregnant and cuddling a dog. She was in her late twenties, a former prostitute, one of several Japanese women who had drifted into the world of Kotobuki, which represented a kind of sanctuary for misfits. I mentioned Kazuo's name. 'Do you think he's a bad man?' she asked. I said I didn't think so. 'The Union people are angry with him,' she said, 'because of those photographs. But he's not as bad as they think. He left his things here if you want to take them.' And she pointed to a cardboard box and an old army rucksack, which she was keeping in the corridor because the room was too small. Yuri was friendly, but since Jojo was still at work I didn't stay talking for too long. She directed me to Rogelio's room.

I didn't yet know that everyone in the building had a system of codes for knocking, so that they could all immediately be aware of the presence of a stranger. I heard movements in Rogelio's room, but when I knocked on the door there was a sudden silence. I knocked again. Nothing happened. I waited a few moments, then I began to wonder whether I had made a mistake. A gruff voice – the typical voice (as I later discovered and which I later imitated) of a Filipino pretending to be Japanese – called out, '*Dare?*'

I spoke in our language. 'I'm Rey.'

'Which Rey?'

'Kazuo's friend. We met last year. I saw Ruby in the Philippines and she asked me to contact you.' At the mention of the girl's name he opened the door.

I was about to take my shoes off, but Rogelio told me to bring them inside so that no one would know I was there. He was about five feet tall and his room was just long enough for him to lie down in. The tiny opaque window was tightly closed. I asked him why he didn't open it. He said that the immigration agents sometimes put a ladder to the window to check whether there was a Filipino inside.

I squatted down, and Rogelio lay back on the mat. 'Have you really met Ruby?' he said.

I'd met her in this same room a year before, when she was recovering from an operation for TB, and later in Manila at her sister's home. This had been hard to find. It was in an upstairs room in a squatters' area near the railway track, next door to a junkyard. They called it their studio, but it was small for the purpose, around four metres square, divided off from the cooking area by a curtain of old sacks. The dance floor was covered in green vinyl. There was a turntable and a tape deck, a telephone and a desk. It was here that Ruby's brother-in-law ran a business recruiting and supposedly training dancers for Japan. He offered a package deal – job, passport, all documentation and tickets – for between $1000 and $1500, and he had made enough from this to buy ostentatious jewellery for himself, and to print a calling card giving a business address in a more prosperous part of town.

Ruby had not yet fully recovered, and it seemed to me that she would be unlikely to recover in the heavy pollution of Manila, in this noisy cramped room. Her sister, too, was coughing heavily. They were taking a lot of medicines, without any effect. I told Rogelio how I had advised Ruby to go back to her home in the province if she wanted to recover, but her heart was set on returning to Japan. Her two children were already in the countryside, with their grandmother, and Ruby was determined to go back to the bars of Yokohama.

By now, Rogelio believed my story and he asked if I had anywhere to stay. I told him that, if I could get work the next day, I would find a room. 'You can stay here tonight,' he said, 'if you can bear it.'

The furnishings were minimal: plastic tatami and some bedding, utensils in one corner on the floor, nothing on the walls. Rogelio's possessions were packed in assorted bundles, bags and suitcases, stacked away on the shelves, ready for shipping, perhaps, and ready certainly for any emergency move. There was a tiny electric heater, which did not make much impact on the cold of the room.

Four Pinoys (Filipinos) arrived and Rogelio introduced me in a way which was supposed to be affectionate, although I didn't like it much. 'This is Rey Negro,' he said, 'Koto's latest arrival.' All my nicknames would be to do with the darkness of my skin – Nognog or Tisoy (which means *mestizo*, but in my case *mestizo negro*). To distinguish me from other Reys, I was often referred to, in recollection of this day, as Rey Negro, the adopted son of Rogelio. To the Japanese I was plain *kuroi-hito*, black person.

Rogelio produced a ¥10,000 note and asked one of the men to buy half a case of beer, and I could tell from the way this request was accepted that he must be a figure of some respect. Generous, too. From their accents I could tell that his friends were all his province-mates from Laguna. A whole case of Kirin beer arrived. Chicken livers, smoked fish and grilled intestines were neatly laid out on a newspaper. The first beer was offered to me, and, with the drink, the questions began.

3

The Welcoming Party

'WHERE'S YOUR FRIEND now?' said Rogelio. The
group fell silent. I wondered whether to give them a
straight answer about Kazuo.

'Maybe he's in Tokyo,' I said casually.

Everyone was watching me.

The oldest of the group, Ka Doroy, spoke. 'You tell
him he's stupid. He took our pictures and published
them in an international magazine. They could read
that in our country. They could read it in *America*.'
He gave a certain glamour to the word America as
he spoke. I kept silent, wanting to dissociate myself
from Kazuo.

Actually, although I didn't yet know this, Ka
Doroy loved having his picture taken. Kazuo had
shown him in the act of wrapping a parcel to send
home – an appropriate image since Doroy was an
Odori-boy. Every time there was a flea market in
Odori Park he would be there – his room was a

warehouse of junk, destined for his family back home. He made everyone laugh when he bought a suit, and then an overcoat, and then dark glasses, to complete his outfit for church. Doroy had posed for Kazuo, who had given him a copy of the picture. If anything was wrong, it was the fact that his name wasn't printed underneath.

Rogelio said, 'How did you come to Japan? What's your visa?'

I finished my beer and cleared my throat before explaining. 'I came here with a student visa, but it will expire in a couple of weeks.'

Somebody said, 'How did you manage to get one? Isn't it very difficult?'

'I was a student here last year.'

'So you left your school and came here.'

'No,' I replied, deciding to level with them on this sensitive point. 'After the course, I went home. But I told the people at the airport I was just going for a Christmas holiday. They gave me a re-entry visa.'

Doroy relished the ingeniousness of this. 'You too have got brains,' he said. He was the oldest in the room, and I was the youngest. The implication was that we were the only ones in the room with brains.

The scam over the re-entry visa seemed to satisfy people. Indeed I was a sort of novelty – no one else in Koto had pulled that trick, and I sensed by now that they would probably accept me. But they didn't accept everyone who had a legal visa. Sometimes they wouldn't walk with them on the streets. They resented their freedom. You had to be a bona fide illegal to be one of the group.

Rogelio produced another ¥10,000 and asked Doroy to buy more beer, and this surprised me for two reasons. It was an odd thing to do to the oldest man in the room – in the *barrio* it could be a terrible insult. Here it implied that Rogelio was in command, and that Doroy was being treated as an honorary young man. Buying beer was a kid's job, and Doroy relished it. He didn't like the name Doroy, which had implications of old age. He preferred to be called Jun (for Junior). Acting the young man was important for him, for his survival in a context to which he was not well fitted. The work was hard for him and he knew no Japanese. He needed the cooperation of the group, and he couldn't rely on that if he behaved like the grandfather that he was.

The second reason for surprise was the way these people spent their money. Before I arrived in Koto I had the notion that life there was simply a matter of loneliness and exploitation, and the continual pressure to remit money home. This was the way it had been written up in dozens of articles about migrant workers. But the subjects of these articles didn't always resemble their portraits, as I was beginning to see.

Ruffino, for instance, who at the beginning of the

drinking session had at first pleaded a hangover, then protested he would never touch a drink again. He was the only one of the group who could get drunk Japanese style – even Koto style, which meant falling asleep on the pavement, or wherever you happened to be. Always red-eyed, he wore a balaclava helmet and dark glasses. In this disguise he looked Japanese. He would drink *sake* or *shochu* with the Japanese day-labourers, drinks which the rest of the Pinoys disliked. The only thing he couldn't do was speak Japanese, otherwise he had been pretty well assimilated. As for his family back home, it was said that he hadn't sent any money for two years. Now he sat there, sizing me up and giving paternal advice – take whatever job is available, don't be choosy, save your money . . .

When Doroy returned, the others began prodding him to tell his story. He had been here four years, and his passport was due to expire the next month, but he was unwilling to go to the Philippine embassy, because they might report him to Immigration, or try to convince him to surrender.

A little beer made him boastful. He squatted on the tatami, propping his elbow familiarly on Ruffino's knee. He had assumed the manner of a village elder, but at the same time he dropped all formality and addressed me as his mate, even though he was older than my father. The others had all heard his stories a hundred times before, but still they egged him on.

'You may not believe it,' he said, stabbing the air with his finger, 'but I have thirteen children by five women.' I resisted a smile. 'I'm not lying! I have one in Ilocos Sur, one in Bacolod City, one in Quiapo, one in Pangasinan and one in Baclaran. These are the mothers of my children,' he said, pointing emphatically at the tatami. 'I love all my children, but not their mothers. I'll support them to the end of my life. To the end of my life! However much I suffer here in Japan. When I get back home, I'll see to it that we have this grand reunion.'

'Will you invite their mothers?' I asked.

'Not at first,' said Ka Doroy, sipping his beer. He was still on his first bottle, and he only drank to be one of the boys. 'I'll visit the mothers one by one. You may think I'm already old at fifty-five, but I tell you, I can still get an erection. I'll bet you one month's earnings if you want.'

By now Ruffino's face had sunk onto the tatami. Rogelio sucked his teeth and said authoritatively, 'Not any more. Ka Doroy can't get an erection any more.'

Doroy ignored him. 'I tell you,' he continued, concentrating his attention on me,' I can still make a woman come. I prefer them in their thirties, especially if they're widows. I don't like young girls. Widows are more experienced.'

A little later he said, 'I haven't made love in four years. It's very expensive, ¥30,000 minimum, as much as your week's savings. You can have young girls too if you want. I saw them in the magazines. Some of them don't even have pubic hairs.'

It was now too cold to go out for more beer, and the group broke up, leaving Rogelio and myself. Rogelio had a wife and three children in the Philippines, but since he was far from home he reckoned he could do as he pleased.

So he had taken up with Ruby. The saddest thing, he told me, was that Ruby had been tricked into prostitution by the family business – not by the brother-in-law, with his gold rings and his calling card, but by his sister, whom, as it happened, I had also met.

Mrs Recto was an expensive person to have dealings with. I knew another family on whom she had inflicted disaster. They had borrowed $2,500 to send their son, Crispin, to Japan. On arrival he had found himself engaged in construction work for the Yakuza, and earning practically nothing. He was in Chiba prefecture, at the mercy of his employers, unable to remit money, practically starving. A Filipina took pity on him and adopted him for a few weeks, before introducing him to Kotobuki. He had been in Japan for just over a year when he died on the way to the jobsite, supposedly of heart failure. He was only twenty-four.

At the time that I met her, Mrs Recto was a little worried. Crispin's family were not satisfied with the story of their son's death, and they were trying to get her to help them recover the body. I didn't tell her what I knew about her, and the business she ran from a room in an Ermita hotel, but within a few minutes of conversation she told me something striking about herself: that her Japanese husband had also died of heart failure, while they were making love.

She was large, ugly and sexy, a manipulative woman with a helpful manner. If I hadn't known about Crispin, I could easily imagine myself trusting her, as she handed me her Japanese address and told me to call her if ever I needed a job. The job she fixed up for Ruby turned out to be in a *casa*, a type of brothel where the girls are locked into their rooms. Ruby had been stuck there for a month, before a Japanese customer, hearing her story, paid the 'fine' for taking her out for the evening and had helped her to escape.

Arriving in Kotobuki, still plump and healthy, she had fallen for another trick, this time inflicted on her by Rogelio. One night he treated her to a disco, after which they walked, by a long detour, to one of the love hotels I had passed that afternoon. There, Rogelio told Ruby that if she didn't go with him he would leave her outside on the street. Not knowing Yokohama, she was unaware that she was only five minutes' walk from her lodging. She would curse herself afterwards for having been so easily taken in.

But the match was a success and she had reason to be grateful to Rogelio when, a little later, she discovered she had TB. At first she refused to be hospitalised, for fear the immigration people would find her. But Rogelio persuaded her, and spent most of his money on her bills. She was also helped by one of the informal support groups which deal with migrant workers. But she lost one lung, and finally had to give herself up to the authorities.

Almost every other day, Rogelio received letters from Ruby, more than he received from his wife, and the letters, he said, were more beautiful to read. She always remembered their happy days together, and she would even tell him not to fuck too much because his 'bird' would get worn out and there would be nothing for her, or for his wife. 'Every night,' Rogelio said drowsily, 'she would dance naked in front of me, until I could no longer contain myself.' He could last, he said, up to seven 'explosions'.

Having said this, he fell silent and was soon snoring. But I was unable to sleep. I was too cold, excited and afraid. Tomorrow I would find work in Kotobuki.

4

A Standing Man

ROGELIO, WHO HAD a regular job and therefore didn't need to get up early and compete, directed me to the Centre, telling me to look out for other Pinoys and stick with them. What everyone called the Centre was nothing more than an intersection on Kotobuki-cho where, at five in the morning, about a hundred workers were milling around, buying food from the noodle shops and stores, and eating their breakfast on the street.

These were the *tachimbo*, the Standing Men, day-labourers dependent on the casual system of hire. The Japanese gathered on one corner of the intersection, drinking sake, beer or cans of coffee from the vending machine. They were a pathetic sight, and it was clear that many of them were not interested in working that day – some of them were not in their working clothes, others were sitting on the pavement. If you wanted to be hired, you must show that you were worth hiring. Standing, not sitting, was part of the deal.

Elsewhere there were Pakistanis, Sri Lankans and one Latino, as well as the Filipinos scattered around the four corners of the intersection. I discovered later that this technique of spreading out was part of a strategy in case of raids. The aim was partly to remain inconspicuous. But there was also the fact that, whenever we gathered in a group, we would automatically become very noisy. That would cause complaints.

Although I was hungry, I was too anxious about finding work to spend any time buying food. I greeted the Latino with 'Buenos dias' and he replied with a smile. The Filipino standing next to him paid no attention to us, but he was too close for me to ignore him politely. Could he give me any tips on how to behave in front of a *sacho*? Who were they? What did they look like?

The term *sacho*, literally manager or boss, meant in this context the recruiter or middleman who would give us a job. Dodong, the Filipino, told me just to follow him when the sacho came.

A plump figure in green gabardine trousers and dark glasses, his hair slicked back and his head held at a superior tilt, rushed passed Dodong. 'OK,' he said, 'come on you three,' and he pointed to a bus across the street. I asked him what our work was going to be. It was a bold question. Kazuo had told me always to ask, in case it was at some dangerous chemical works. But most people didn't ask, because if you asked too many questions you risked not being hired. The sacho was dismissive. 'I don't know yet,' he said, 'eight hours, twelve thousand.' He didn't tell us where we would be going.

We waited half an hour in the bus while the sacho darted around looking for more people. He needed anybody he could get, but another bus had taken most of the Filipinos. I'd seen fewer of them than I had expected. There were other vehicles on side-streets waiting to pick them up, and those with regular jobs knew the exact pick-up points in advance.

In the end there were only Japanese drunks left on the street, and a group of down-and-outs around a fire. The sacho had been looking for young people, which meant Filipinos or other foreigners. But apart from Dodong, the Latino (a Columbian called William) and myself, all he could find was Japanese, many of them in their sixties.

I sat with William, and watched Dodong from a distance. He seemed completely at ease, a veteran. The journey took around three hours, and all the time I was worried that we might be destined for some dangerous construction site or chemical factory. When we stopped at a noodle restaurant, neither Dodong nor I could keep up with the speed at which the Japanese bolted their food. I tried to eat fast, but Dodong couldn't care less. 'Slow down,' he said. 'They can wait a few minutes for us.'

We drove on along the coast, through a landscape dotted with empty containers and piles of wooden pallets, with occasional clusters of warehouses by the wharves, and a sea that looked at first black, then an unpleasant, chemical green. Everywhere, gigantic cranes crisscrossed the sky. Finally we turned off into the docks and came to a halt at the end of a pier.

The wind from the sea went straight to the bone as we stood on the dockside changing into our working clothes. I put on the warm, light *hatabi* shoes I had borrowed from Akihiro. They wrap around the feet and the lower calf, and the thick cotton is very comfortable.

I looked up at the vast ship we were due to work in. It was from the People's Republic of China. A tattered red flag with five stars was flapping in the wind. The sides of the vessel were streaked with rust and the paint was coming off in scales. I'd never been in a ship before.

Our new sacho, a tall man with a towel wrapped around his head, led us up the gangway, from which we could see that the ship was loaded with mountains of brownish granules. One of the Japanese told me they were used for making fertiliser. We climbed down the ladder into the hold, and were given spades. Our job was to shovel those of the granules that could not be reached by the bulldozers, and my first reaction was that this would not be such a hard job. After all, I grew up in the paddyfields and was used to digging ditches and irrigation canals.

At first I couldn't see how the crane, with its huge scoop, was operated. It seemed to think for itself, grabbing at a great load of granules, releasing them again if they were too much, grabbing again, screeching as it went. Then I noticed a figure above us, a fat bald old man with a remote control in a yellow box. Below, the bulldozers went into action, roaring like tanks, piling up the granules for the scoop.

The drivers were unsmiling, and they worked their machines recklessly, tearing at the ribs of the ship so that sparks flew. We worked in the spaces between the ribs, shovelling out the granules that remained, deafened by the bulldozers. The worst moments came when we were close to the crane, or if the bulldozer passed close behind us as we worked. It was the thought of the cable snapping, or of being pinned under the caterpillar tracks. And as the day went on, there was another fear: what if, from sheer fatigue, I fell down the hatch ladder?

The Japanese workers kept a close watch on the time. After four hours we were given lunch-boxes on the dockside – rice, meat and pickles. It was only when we broke off for supper that Dodong told me the whole nature of the deal. Since supper was free, that meant there would be overtime. If there was overtime, that meant we would simply work on until the job was finished.

But the job was very far from finished. Masses of granules remained. The Japanese muttered over their food. Nobody could complain and neither William nor Dodong wanted to. The more work, the more money.

Two powerful floodlights were positioned on the side of the ship. The place felt like a concentration camp, and as midnight passed the sacho kept urging us to work faster. By now the Japanese were beginning to flag, and when the sacho wasn't looking they would take a rest in the ribs of the ship. I wanted to prove myself a good worker, so I would be hired again, but movement itself was agony, and sometimes I found myself working with my eyes closed. I could have lain down on the spot and fallen fast asleep. When the work was finally complete, at one in the morning, I could hardly climb back up the ladder for pain. I pissed on the deck, too exhausted to walk first to the shore. It was excruciatingly cold, and everyone else was rushing to the bus.

The day, which had begun at five, ended at three the next morning, when we picked up our wages from the sacho's office in Yokohama. I opened the thin brown envelope at once. It contained ¥25,000 – almost two hundred dollars by the exchange rate of the time.

'It's not enough,' said Dodong. 'I think the Japanese got more than we did.'

'It's a lot,' I said.

'Should have been three *lapad*,' said Dodong – thirty thousand.

We started walking toward Kotobuki, the only people out on the street, obvious *gaijin*, foreigners, in our dirty work-clothes. 'Aren't there any police here?' I asked.

Dodong wasn't worried about the *parak*, as he called them in our slang. He was keeping to the side-streets, where we were less conspicuous among the poplars. But when we came to the road he told me to hurry up.

He had agreed to let me spend the rest of the night in his room but first he had a meal waiting for him. We passed Convenience, the 24-hour store, and arrived at Dodong's building. Gently, he slid the front door open and we entered like thieves.

He knocked twice at one of the ground-floor rooms and called the name of Margie. When she opened the door, a gust of perfume hit me full in the face. She gave us a good welcome, as if there were nothing odd about the timing of our visit. Dodong's food was waiting for him, and he didn't want to waste it. I was impressed that he felt he could call on Margie at any time of the night. He seemed a single-minded individual – he was planning to go back to work in a few hours. Margie fitted in,

31

unquestioningly, with his arrangement. Concealing her sleepiness, she dished up the pork adobo and rice, even offering to heat it up if that was what Dodong wanted.

I ate a little, out of politeness, but the unventilated room with its overwhelming smell of perfume began to give me a headache. I hadn't realised that there were Filipinas in Kotobuki, and I couldn't quite place Margie. When we rose to leave, she suggested that I should take my meals with her in the future.

5

The Queen of Koto

DURING THE NEXT few days, while I was staying back in Tokyo but working in Kotobuki, Akihiro's landlord discovered what was going on, and told him that the contract would have to be changed and that he would have to pay more. Very politely, Akihiro explained this to me, and the next day, very politely, I removed my rucksack from his room and set off to look for lodgings in Kotobuki.

Margie opened the door to me, and once again I gagged on the stench of cheap perfume. When I explained my plan, Margie immediately offered to help and we went to see the landlord together. I couldn't have chosen a better ally. One of the first things you noticed about Margie was her breasts, which she deployed eloquently. The further she leant over the counter, the more she revealed. She spoke in a primitive, telegraphic Japanese, with an affected shyness that was very sexy and sweet. The more she flirted, the more stiff and business-like the landlord became, and there was something about the way he refused to acknowledge the flirtation that made me realise the message had got across. Margie and Frank (as he liked to be called by us) had an understanding.

It turned out that a room was due to be vacated that evening, and until then Margie suggested I wait in her room, where, with hardly a moment lost, she began telling me her life story. She had married at the age of fourteen and had eight children by the time she was twenty-four. Her husband had been fifteen years older than her, 'old enough to be my father'. He was a sadist, she said. He beat her every day. He had even struck her mother. So she had left him after the birth of the last child. She was still young and beautiful then, she said, but her problem was she didn't know how to cook. Oh, she could fry things, but that was all. Her husband hadn't liked this.

Husband number two was a policeman. That had lasted ten years. No child. But the policeman was unfaithful, so she moved on to husband number three, with whom she stayed for five years, until he made a close friend of hers pregnant. At this point, Margie decided to have her virginity restored, which she did at a cost of one thousand dollars. That had come as a big surprise to husband number four, her current – that she should be as tight as *that* at her age. On their first night he had shaken his head in disbelief, and she had laughed to herself at the brilliance of the deception, at the wonders of science.

Husband number four was due soon in Japan. In the meantime, the man in the next room seemed to be falling for her . . .

Margie showed me photos of her eight children, some of whom were now living in Canada, and their letters begging her to emigrate there and to give up Japan. But she said, 'I have my world, my children have theirs. I am happy with my life.'

While she was telling me this story, Margie prepared a meal, frying fish, eggs and pork chops on her electric stove in the corridor. Her neighbour Daisy joined us, and the flow of intimacies continued. Both women spoke without inhibition, in a style which I wasn't used to – Daisy's continual swearing, Margie's gynaecological details. They made me laugh. I wondered about Margie's motives. With the landlord, she had been a plain flirt. With me she was both seductive and motherly.

She was casually dressed in tracksuit bottoms, and her cleavage showed prominently under a sweatshirt. Her hair had been tinted brown and her face was heavily made up. It was swollen and lumpy, without any trace of past beauty. Her eyes seemed to signal a mixture of spontaneous compassion and calculation. I didn't ask her or Daisy what they did for a living, because I already had a fairly good idea.

They were what the Japanese mass media call *Japayuki-san* - Miss Japan-Bound girls (an adaptation of the term *Karayuki-san*, Miss China-bound, referring to the prostitutes who served the Japanese Imperial Army). The Karayuki-san came to the Philippines during the Occupation, and some years ago if you referred to a woman as a *Haponesa*, that meant she was a prostitute. Now that perception has been reversed. If the Japanese see a Filipina in their country, they automatically assume that she's on the job. In fact not all of them are. Some are maids for foreigners. Some have married farmers (who find it practically impossible to attract Japanese girls to the country life). Many are legitimate entertainers, waiting in bars, singing to the karaoke when requested. A few are students.

Nevertheless, many of the girls who go out as entertainers end up as prostitutes, and many others know exactly what the deal is from the start. Most prostitution in Manila caters for Filipinos rather than foreigners. Girls working in this area would naturally be attracted by the thought that they can earn in one day in Japan what would take them a month in Manila. So they go to the so-called Dance Studios and Promotion Agencies which operate throughout the main cities of the Philippines. There they get fixed up with jobs as 'cultural dancers' or 'artistes', for a 'budget' of between $300 and $800 a month, according to their beauty and abilities. Naturally this is an exploitation wage. The rest is made up by prostitution.

The contracts these girls receive tie them to work at a particular bar, where they are given special lodgings, and where they are strictly guarded. The *casa* in which Ruby had worked, a sort of sex prison, was exceptional, and it was later raided by the authorities. But now there are the Live Shows in Tokyo and Yokohama, where the girls have sex on stage. These are also illegal, in theory. Both in the Philippines and in Japan, the recruitment of the girls is the province of the Yakuza. They make a tour of the agencies, picking out the girls they want. It is mostly the Yakuza who channel the money back to the agencies.

I never spoke directly to Daisy and Margie about their work. In the afternoons, after a visit to the public bath, they would make their preparations for the evening, which began at six. When they emerged from their rooms, they were transformed: high heels, tight-fitting pants, revealing blouses, spray-netted hair and – what made them almost unrecognisable – the manner of their walk. It was fragile and dignified, as if they were rising to the occasion.

I would watch Margie from my window on the fifth floor, making her immaculate way. She once told me that what she liked most about Japan was the fact that, when you walk along the street, you don't get dust on your face, unlike in Manila. Her evening sorties were designed to attract attention, a metamorphosis, a royal event.

In time, I got to know all her four boyfriends. They called her *Reyna ng Kotobuki*, the Queen of Koto, or *Asawa ng Bayan*, the People's Wife – for she was wife, or mother, or both, to everybody.

6

How Arguments Begin

WILLIAM, THE LATINO, had found a job which paid ¥12,000 a day, instead of the ¥8,000 I was getting as a *dokata-boy*, a navvy. I went to see him at his lodgings, to ask him to cut me in on the deal. While we were talking in the doorway, an argument broke out between two drunken Filipinos further down the corridor. One was trying to close the door of his room, but his attacker had his hand on the knob and was brandishing a small kitchen knife. They lunged at each other like Samurais.

The man with the knife eventually gave up and came past us, muttering as he ran downstairs, 'If only I had a bigger knife.' At this point the unarmed man locked his room and left it. 'Don't tell him where I am,' he begged me, as he disappeared upstairs.

A moment later, the other man returned with a *beinte-nueve*, or butterfly knife. He took one look at the closed door, then turned on me. 'He's your mate, isn't he?' he said, holding the blade as if ready to plunge it into my throat.

'No, no, no,' I screamed. 'I'm a newcomer in Kotobuki. I don't know him. Believe me.'

The man had a coarse, cratered face and a bushy moustache. He seemed to be sizing me up. Then he glanced along the corridor and suddenly decided to check the fire-escape. At this point an older man appeared, agitated and with a cigarette in his trembling hand. He grabbed my umbrella and raised it as if to hit me in the face. 'He's your mate, isn't he?' he said.

I repeated that I knew nothing of the man.

'You lying son of a whore. He's your mate.'

'No, I'm a student. I'm a newcomer.' With a single blow the older man scattered all the books and magazines I was carrying. I begged William to let me into his room, but he quickly retreated and bolted the door. Now I was crying. The older man continued to curse and threaten me, while the one with the knife kept searching for his enemy.

I produced my blue card and pleaded that I was a student and had nothing to do with whatever the quarrel had been. The card had no affect on him, but his mate reappeared and said, 'Quick. Let's get out of here. He may have called his friends.' And the two disappeared.

The floor of the corridor was wet. I picked up my papers. William's door remained shut. If there was a gang-fight in the offing, he didn't want to have anything to do with us. I walked fast in the direction of home, then began to run, scared that I might meet the two again. By the time I reached the building, I was breathing like a tired bull.

I didn't want to go to my room, in case they somehow tracked me down. Dodong would be at work. The only friend I had was Margie.

Her door was open and she was talking to some people in the corridor. As I approached they turned around and I got a nasty shock. It was the same two men.

This time they looked at me with complete indifference. I could see the knife in the younger man's back pocket. The two were pacing nervously around the corridor, drawing on their cigarettes. It took me a second or two to realise that they simply didn't recognise me. Indeed they completely accepted my presence. If I was a friend of Margie I was a friend of theirs.

Margie was asking what had been going on. It was nothing, they said, a simple problem, 'a little knot'. Then Margie noticed a slight scratch on the young man's hand. 'What happened to that?'

'Oh, somebody just scratched it . . . ' He paused, then couldn't hold back the curse. 'Son of a whore impakto!' An *impakto* is a kind of witch with long fingernails.

Margie said soothingly, 'You know, sometimes

it's better here to be a coward than a brave man. If you're a coward you won't get into trouble. It's just between us Filipinos. Nothing good will become of us if you keep on doing this.'

'If he doesn't leave Kotobuki we'll get him, son of a whore.'

I was gently backing away, still fearful that they might recognise me, when the old man turned to me and said, 'Want a cigarette, mate?'

I'd never smoked. 'Yes,' I said, and took one of his Philip Morris's. I did all the things that smokers do. I wanted to spit, but couldn't.

Margie continued giving her soothing advice. It was a quarrel over jobs, typical of the kind of quarrel that would flare up in Koto and that could lead straight to a knifing. In this case, the man with the knife thought he had been purposely excluded from a jobsite by his mate. It wasn't true, and in a few days the matter had been forgotten. Just as these murderous confrontations could come at you from nowhere, so they could vanish with a swift, casual reconciliation.

I couldn't bear to finish the cigarette. When I thought the two were sufficiently calm, I turned to the older man and said, 'Do you recognise me, sir? I'm the one you almost hit with an umbrella.'

'Really?' he said blankly, and his mind wandered off onto something else. I went up to my room. A few days later, when I was working with the young man, I told of the moment when he had pointed his knife at my neck. 'Really?' he said, with that same blank casualness. 'Sorry, mate.'

I was working with Akihiro. During a break we were rehearsing some exercises we had learnt from our shaolin lessons. Juan, Margie's neighbour, came up to me. 'If you know so much about martial arts,' he said, 'don't do it here. Do it outside.' There was a challenge implied, which I avoided.

Juan was married with children, but his wife was paralysed. Indeed, Margie told me she was already a vegetable. Although he was the butt of many jokes, Juan himself never laughed or smiled. He was always deep in thought and usually went by himself.

After the incident at work I was having supper in Margie's room as usual when Juan returned. 'Are you ready for your meal?' said Margie. Juan replied that he would change his clothes first, and from this simple exchange, and the fact that he didn't acknowledge my presence, I knew at once that he was the man Margie had mentioned as having fallen for her, and that he didn't like my presence in the room.

He returned a few minutes later and Margie introduced me. 'Oh yes,' he said, 'we were working on the same barge today.' In fact we had been together for two weeks. He was the Filipino sacho, choosing the men who worked with him. He took his place on the tatami in a proprietorial manner and proceeded to ignore me. Margie produced a large bowl of food and administered to him meekly and appeasingly. He ate slowly, as if without much appetite. I left quickly.

The next evening at supper Dodong told Margie he had bought a new radio cassette player, and he invited us to his room on the fifth floor. There we were joined by Romero, a neighbour from across the way – a tall, handsome man in his late twenties.

Dodong went on about the virtues of his new acquisition, which he had bought cheap and which looked to me like a fake. Romero fiddled with the controls, and Margie leant forward to examine the machine, full of compliments.

They weren't flirting. They weren't even looking at each other. But there was something unnatural about the way they sat together, as if there were an implied limit to their intimacy. I smiled as I watched Margie. She was in what we call the dog position, which a woman would not normally adopt without a purpose, and she kept finding new things to say about the indifferent machine.

There was a loud knock and Margie sat upright. We all froze, thinking the same thing. Then Dodong muttered that it was too early for the police. He reached for the knob and pushed the door open.

Juan surveyed us all briefly from the corridor. He was in a rage. He turned to Margie with a sneer. 'Ah, you're here,' he said. 'What are you doing here?' Before she could reply he had pulled her to her feet.

44

'What's this?' she said, resisting.

'A woman shouldn't come to a man's place,' he said, dragging her from the room like a pig to the slaughter.

'You're shaming me,' she cried. 'What right have you to do this?'

Margie began wailing and, as she was dragged along the corridor, the Japanese neighbours opened their doors in turn.

'Why don't you do something,' I said to Romero and Dodong. I was thinking that Romero was big enough to tackle Juan easily.

Romero clucked his tongue. 'Let's not interfere with their private lives,' he said. The incident seemed nothing special to him.

Later, after Romero had left the room, I asked Dodong why Juan had been so angry, and he explained that Margie used to be Romero's *bata* (literally his 'child', the word we use for a girlfriend). But Romero was casual with his partners. When he dropped them, he dropped them just like that. Margie had now been Juan's bata for the best part of a year, but he hadn't forgotten about her past. And he didn't like her visiting the fifth floor.

But Margie had no intention of being one man's exclusive property, and she had her own way of dealing with this problem.

7

Juan, Margie, Miguel

WE WERE WORKING on a ship owned by KDD, the large communications company, who were laying new telephone lines to the States. It was very easy work – simply a matter of coiling cables around a big winch in the hold. Boring work too, but we all wanted it.

The *teheishi*, the recruiter subcontracted by KDD, regularly needed a dozen people, and Juan, overcoming his lack of Japanese, had persuaded him to let him find the workers. This had put Juan in a unique position – he was the only Filipino sacho at the time. He still worked alongside us, but it was he who gave us our wages at the end of the day.

He would sit beside the teheishi in the van on the way back from work, and hand out the packets of cash. But he soon arranged it so that he wouldn't be given the money in front of us, which meant we never knew how much he was getting. Sometimes there was an allowance for lunch, sometimes not.

He couldn't hide the pleasure his new power gave him, and he particularly liked ordering me around, me being the youngest, a newcomer, not a gang member, and therefore vulnerable. It was not long before he explained that I should be grateful to him for having given me work: I should give him something, he said.

But I didn't give him anything.

After the incident in Dodong's room I had stopped eating at Margie's. Juan's jealousy made things uncomfortable, and anyway, I was paying over the odds for the food. Margie had left it up to me to contribute what I wanted, and this had put me in an awkward position. I didn't want to seem tight-fisted, so I paid a thousand a day. In a cheap restaurant I could escape Margie's endless fried food and eat well for five hundred. So I pretended to her that, not wanting to disturb her, I was now cooking for myself.

One evening I met her in the hall. She was dressed up in tight white jeans and a revealing red V-neck jumper.

'I haven't seen you for a week,' she said. 'I've been looking for you because I wanted to pay back the five thousand I borrowed.'

I ignored that. I knew she'd been avoiding me. And I didn't mind about the money. I'd received enough kindnesses from her.

'What happened to your eyes?' I said. 'You must have been crying all night.' Her face was swollen under the mask of make-up.

'We were kicked out of our jobs. Teresa quarrelled with the papa-san. She's only been there four days. She thinks he's a dictator, giving orders without a please or thank-you. I can't blame her. She's new. I've been there a year now and I know his attitude.'

A large man with a *contrabida* face – the face of the leading bad guy in the films – emerged from Margie's room, combing his hair with self-satisfaction and obviously dressed for an evening out.

'This is Rey,' said Margie quickly, as if to tell him not to hit me. 'He's a good man. I owe him five thousand.'

Miguel, the newcomer, paid little attention to me, and I was glad. He was much bigger than me, and he had a gangster look that said: Don't cross my path. I knew that Margie had telephoned him after her quarrel with Juan, and had asked him over to rescue her. More than that, I knew that Miguel had an old quarrel with Dodong, and I had heard a rival gang telling Dodong to report to them if Miguel did anything against him.

Margie was full of kindness, both as a mother and as a lover, but she knew how to protect herself. Miguel had come over, she said, to 'hunt' Juan. But Juan lived next door to her. Miguel was also a lover of hers, of long standing. So now Margie had at least three lovers in the building, excluding the landlord. It was like a chess manoeuvre.

Miguel, Margie and I walked out of the building. Juan and Dodong were standing by the vending machine. I walked in their direction. Nothing was said until Miguel, a short way off, looked back over his shoulder and gave the two of them a brief, threatening look. Then Dodong muttered softly, *"tang 'na mo'* – your mother is a whore.

Wherever they go, Filipinos organise and divide themselves according to place of origin. In Kotobuki, the Bataan group, from Central Luzon, was the strongest and most feared. The saying was, 'Don't fight with the men from Bataan.' They were the ones most often involved in stabbings. Their strength derived in part from the fact that they had been the pioneers of the Filipino community. Kotobuki, ten years before, had been the place where seamen went to await their ships, or to stay between jobs. As they ran out of money, they took to unofficial work. Later, people got into the habit of jumping ship there. In the mid-Eighties, as the yen appreciated, the influx grew. The Bataan group was already firmly entrenched.

The second notorious group called themselves in English 'The Intruders' or 'The Intruders in Japan'. They came from Muntinlupa, south of Manila. They were famous for their hit-men, or *tiradores*. They were street-fighters, and they held sway in their territories by means of an alliance with the Laguna and Pampanga factions.

The biggest group, and the best organised, was not based on place of origin but on religion. The *Iglesia ni Kristo*, a native Filipino religion founded in 1914, claims a membership of five million. They deny the divinity of Christ. They have a strict system of tithes, which has made the church extremely wealthy. They are not supposed to drink or smoke.

In Japan, the *Iglesia* had GIs of Filipino origin at Atsugi American Air Force base in Yokohama, which gave them PX privileges. So they had a legal basis for their community. They could hold church services and parties at Atsugi. In Kotobuki, where they were illegal workers like the rest, they were absolutely exclusive. They had their own corner of the street where they waited for jobs. Each member or newcomer was given help in finding employment, even woken up if there was a vacancy going. It was impossible to get on their list, and this caused trouble. But if you fought with an Iglesia you made an enemy of the whole church. They would come to your room in a gang and threaten you.

I am an Ilokano from Northern Luzon, but as yet I didn't know many of my province-mates.

Juan, the 'Filipino sacho', was from the first group. He was from Bataan.

I went with my new friend Manny to await the

work-bus. We expected no problem, since the KDD teheishi had asked us the night before to show up. But the bus failed to arrive. After thirty minutes, Manny and I became suspicious. We searched among the likely places in Kotobuki, and eventually found the van parked just in front of our own building. It was already filled with Filipinos, most of them new to me. Juan was seated in front.

We got in, without saying a word to Juan. The teheishi greeted us. Then Juan started the headcount. There were thirteen of us, and only a dozen jobs. Someone would have to take a *yasumi*, a rest.

Ronny Omise, Ronny the Bar, was one of the toughest old-timers in Kotobuki. He thought of himself as the Filipino *oyabun*, Yakuza's boss, and although he was not exactly that, it would be hard for Juan to bully him. Ronny the Bar said, 'Juan, why don't *you* take yasumi? You were working last night.'

So there was a night-shift now. We hadn't been told this.

'No,' said Juan, 'I am needed today.' He looked as if he could do with a yasumi. He was half asleep already. 'You take it Rey,' he said.

I argued against this, saying that I was part of the original group and, besides, the sacho liked my work.

The night-shift workers had another Filipino sacho, Ramboy, the man who had pointed a knife at my neck. He too was yawning heavily, and he eventually agreed to step down. But before he left the bus he said to me, 'Next time, you give others a chance.'

Fuck you, I thought.

Out of the twelve of us, eight were from Bataan. Juan had two reasons for hiring them. First they were his province-mates. Second, it was easier for him to cheat them, as we found out at the end of the day when he gave us ¥10,000, ¥2,000 short. Meanwhile his mates would owe him a debt of gratitude for finding them an easy job.

That day there was a need for overtime, but Manny and I were immediately excluded. Manny said, 'Our country has never progressed because of people like Juan. As soon as we get a chance for a fast buck, we sacrifice our countrymen for our own selfish interest.' Juan was the type who would one day become mayor of his town. He would be overflowing with benevolence, providing employment – for his wife, his brothers and sisters and maybe even his grandparents.

He told me the following day that only six people were needed. I asked why I wasn't on the list. He gave the standard reply: 'Give the others a chance.' I went off with Manny to find a different job. There was nothing going, and eventually we came across Juan and his group waiting for the bus. When it came, eight of them got in. The teheishi, who needed two more, beckoned us to get in.

'Why did you lie to me?' I said to Juan. He couldn't reply.

And here was a surprise. Miguel, who was still living with Margie was also on the bus. I thought he was supposed to be hunting for Juan. Instead, Juan recognising *force majeure*, had appeased him with a job – my job. Margie had negotiated the deal – man to man it would have been impossible. This made Juan the laughing-stock of the *gemba*, the jobsite. But the deal lasted. Miguel was always on the list, and he lost no time in trying to take over the sacho-ship from Juan.

By the end of that job, all of Margie's boy-friends and exes (the distinction wasn't clear) had worked together – Romero, the one we called the fashion model, Miguel of the Rotten Teeth, and Juan the Monk (the one with a bald patch). Juan's room and Margie's became the social centre for the Bataan group, where they made deals of increasing secrecy. One time, I happened to be on the street looking for a job when the van for the KDD work arrived. There was no one around, but suddenly it was like an ambush. They sprang from their hiding places and jumped into the vehicle.

Juan's luck expressed itself in gold. At mass every Sunday, he appeared with more and more jewellery. He could be persuaded to buy cases of beer for his mates, or coffees all round. But eventually the social life of the Bataan group got them thrown out of the building.

I saw Margie only a few times after that. Once, she had a new diamond ring. Once there was a Canon Instamatic. 'Guess who gave me this,' she would say. I would smile. 'Juan gave this to me,' and her voice would melt. 'He's *very* kind.'

8

Kotobuki Sketchbook

EVERYONE IN KOTO knows that Lando has a student visa, and they envy him his freedom. For instance, he can go out on to the street to use the telephone, without having to keep looking out for police cars. He doesn't have to take taxis rather than walk home, as we often do. Sometimes he deliberately provokes us, taking out his blue card and fanning himself with it. Once a week he goes to Japanese language school. The rest of the time he's an illegal worker.

I try not to let anyone see my notebook. Over lunch, Lando noticed me jotting something down. 'What are you writing?' he asked suspiciously.

'A diary,' I said.

'Why? Are you about to die?'

'I don't know,' I said. 'Maybe. Maybe I'll die tomorrow.'

This is not my country. And I cannot laugh aloud

as I want. I have to observe the etiquette, culture and traditions of this society. I cannot sing my favourite song when I'm happy, but I can weep when I'm angry or lonely. I am alone in this bus, together with seven Japanese. I want to hum a melody. Nobody is stopping me, but this is not my country. This is my second week as a day-labourer. I want to quit. I want to go home.

There were two of us on a barge, unloading huge granite blocks. My partner was a fat, limping old man whom I called *oji-chan*, grandfather. Our job was to fix the cable around the stones and slip the loop onto the hook of the crane. The blocks passed overhead. Each had its weight painted on the side – anything between four and six metric tons. I prayed that Japanese technology would be infallible. I was too scared to work well. The crane operator shouted: '*Fuiripinjin dame yo.*' The Filipino's no good. Then he imperiously held out a hand towards me. '*Pasuporuto?*'

'*Doosta no?*' Why?

He didn't answer.

'*Anata keisatsu ja nai!*' I said. You're not a policeman.

From my room on the fifth floor I can see the greater part of Kotobuki and Yokohama City. It is dawn. Koto is already littered with day-labourers and their half-pint glasses of sake. At every corner, groups gather around charcoal braziers. Others are milling around the pachinko parlours, looking at yesterday's racing results. An old man is feeding breadcrumbs to the pigeons. The Korean shop is doing a brisk trade in gloves and alcohol. Beside the news-stand, the same hemiplegic Yakuza stands playing dice every day, stuffing his takings into a plastic cup. The labourers always complain that they never win, but they are drunk, and so they go on playing. An accomplice keeps an eye out for the police, and the board can be folded in a trice. To my right stands the Yakuza building, three storeys, painted black, with mirrored windows and the name of the gang painted in large gold characters. A black Mercedes outside, and a black Lincoln Continental. They love large black American cars. I don't know what they do in the building.

The Standing Men are like prostitutes. Our customers are discriminating – they size us up. They like us young and strong, muscular but harmless-looking. They don't like a contrabida face. They don't want insolence. If you have long hair, it's better to hide it under a cap, and it's better to be clean-shaven – only the oyabun is permitted a beard. It's important to be seen standing. If you were sitting, that would mean you would just be loafing around on the gemba.

The sachos look us up and down, and we greet

them as politely as we know how. Their method of rejection is not to return our greetings. Every day begins with this little humiliation. We put our lives, unquestioningly, in their hands.

Akihiro and I are at the corner. A drunk approaches me with difficulty and places a steadying hand on my shoulder. 'Fuiripinjin?' he asks, with a smile.

'*Hai, soo desu.*' Yes, I am.

'*Gambare ne!*' Keep it up.

I tell him I will do my best. He walks a little further and meets another drunk. They slump down on the pavement together. The first drunk says, 'I am a very bad man. I am a very bad man. I cannot stop drinking.'

They get up again, holding each other by the shoulders, like a couple of sumo wrestlers. A third drunk is putting coins in the vending machine. 'At least you can still stand up,' he says, 'there's still a chance for you to change yourself.'

Sometimes I wish I didn't know any Japanese at all. The more I understand, the more apprehensive I become. The Japanese day-labourers are beginning to realise that the foreigners, especially the Filipinos, are their potential enemies or competitors. They sneer at us. If you are alone in a work-group they will order you about and make you the butt of their jokes. You have to be understanding and forgiving. We are young and they are old. We're on the way up. They're all but finished.

Yesterday we were given the same wage as our Japanese co-workers. The oldest complained to his companion. He couldn't accept it. He kept shaking his head in disbelief.

Tonight the seven o'clock news had a film report on foreign workers in Japan. It showed Pakistanis and Bangladeshis working at a printing press and mending roads in the rain. It scared me. A storm is brewing. A crackdown is coming.

William and I are walking to church. A policeman on a bicycle comes in the opposite direction down the empty street. William says, 'Just walk straight and pretend not to see him. Maybe he'll think we're seamen.' William was a seaman but he jumped ship. Many sailors, particularly Russians, walk the streets of Kotobuki, looking for junk that's been thrown out.

We do our best to look as if we're on shore leave, with fixed, carefree smiles. The policeman gives us a sideways glance, but passes by.

'I'll tell you one thing,' says William. 'If God is with you, nothing will happen to you. Have faith in God and he will direct you.

I try not to laugh. 'But Señor,' I say, 'God has nothing to do with the police or immigration. If we're arrested, God cannot bribe the police.'

William does not like this line. 'For me,' he says, 'only God knows when to send me back to Colombia.'

Pedro and Cornelio live in the room next door to Margie. They are father and son. Pedro's son-in-law, Teodoro, lives upstairs. They all have wives and children in the Philippines, and they all have lovers here. And there is no secret about it. Cornelio knows that Pedro is being unfaithful to his mother. Pedro knows that Teodore is being unfaithful to his daughter. Back home, this situation would be unthinkable. Here it is quite accepted. They are all men, after all. When Pedro's lover pays her Sunday visit, Cornelio slips out on an errand of his own. During the week, father and son regularly work together.

Pedro was talking with a friend: 'I used to have five *bulitas* when I was in Saudi. I only have one now.'

'What happened to the four?'

'When I first used them,' he said casually, 'my wife cried with pain. She didn't know what was happening.'

'What do you mean?' I asked. I'd heard about bulitas, but I'd always thought it was just a joke.

'Don't you know?' said Pedro with surprise. He unzipped his trousers and showed us his penis, kneeling on the tatami for a prolonged demonstration. Below the glans, there was a lump the size of a pea. He manipulated the skin. 'There's a plastic ball inside,' he said, 'It's hard, made from the stuff they use for screwdriver handles.'

'How do you put it in?'

'There's a Filipino doctor in Saudi. He specialises in this business. We pay him three hundred rials per operation. It's like a circumcision. He injects an anaesthetic into the skin and makes small cuts to insert the bulitas. He puts them just below the surface.'

'Is it painful?' I asked.

'Are you circumcised?' he said mockingly. In the barrios, we are all circumcised around the age of seven. If you're not, you're not a man.

'Yes, I'm circumcised,' I said with some heat.

'It's as painful and itchy as that.'

'Does your wife know now?'

'I showed it to her only after I'd removed the four,' he said, turning the thing to and fro, and tracing where the other bulitas had been. 'It was terribly painful to get rid of them. The skin had grown tight around them. I couldn't get the last one out. Had to give up. I didn't sleep with my wife for two weeks.' Pedro zipped himself up.

'But why do you put them in, anyway?'

The friend said, 'If you can't make your wife happy she'll leave you.'

'So Mang Pedro's wife was unsatisfied.'

'No,' said Pedro,' I wanted to satisfy her more. That's why.'

It's the kind of thing people do in prisons, and Saudi is a prison. Every Sunday, the men get together. They make their own hooch. It's almost impossible to find any sex. They gamble and drink secretly, and they get bored. These operations are carried out in front of the whole group in somebody's flat. It's just something else to do.

Pedro said, 'Everytime I meet my mates in the Philippines, I always ask about their bulitas, and they always say they make their wives more faithful.'

'One day I'll have that done,' said the friend.

'What about you?' said Pedro.

'I think,' I said, 'mine is effective enough.'

A group of Standing Men – Filipinos and Japanese – are waiting on the corner by the vending machines. A drunk Japanese, in his early forties, unshaven and swaggering, comes up. '*Fuiripinjin baka,*' he says to nobody in particular – 'Filipinos are fools.' Tony, an Ilocano of my age, stands near the coffee machine, partially blocking the drunkard's way. He has his hands plunged in his pockets. The drunkard takes the cup of hot coffee, turns to leave and spills some coffee down Tony's arm. '*Aray!*' shouts Tony. Then he leans back and, with some expertise, kicks the drunkard twice in the face and once in the neck. None of us try to restrain Tony, who looks as if he's ready to use his martial arts even further, but an old Japanese man leads the drunkard away. He has sobered up now, and he looks back at Tony in speechless surprise. Then he gets on his bike and rides away.

My immediate reaction is: we Filipinos in Kotobuki are mostly illegals; we are a minority and we suffer discrimination; but if we do things like that, the discrimination will only become worse; fewer and fewer people will want to hire us. We can only lose from this kind of thing. An individual offence here leads automatically to collective guilt. But how can we live without ever expressing our anger or outrage.

Akihiro has been watching the scene. He cannot believe that a foreigner can attack his fellow countryman in his own country. He shakes his head and says, 'Why did he do that to a drunk man? The Filipinos here are a minority. An individual Japanese is weak, but when we group together that guy will be nothing. He'll be a baby.'

9

In and Out
of the Underground

THAT YEAR, JUST as the cherries were coming into blossom, a couple of days before the flower-viewing festival, snow fell on Tokyo. It fell thickly and lay all day on rooftops and in the parks. It dropped in cascades from the trees. It obliterated the flowerbeds. Everywhere there was a scraping of shovels, as the shopkeepers cleared the pavements. The seasons had suddenly gone into reverse and the Tokyo crowd was back in its winter finery – the men in Burberries, the women in tweed.

I felt a complete alien in their midst, with my padded Korean workman's jacket and my borrowed rubber shoes. The crowd looked European to me, and I was in a different uniform, conspicuous for my dark skin among suppressed, sneering smiles and glances. I kicked at the April snow and felt very strange indeed. My visa had expired that day and I was now fully a part of the Filipino underground.

This was the second time I had been involved in an underground and it brought the same sense of paranoia. In the Philippines, during the Marcos years, large numbers of students were part of the resistance to the dictatorship. The degree of our involvement varied: it might be simply a matter of attending rallies and handing out leaflets; it might be candidate membership, or even full membership of the Communist Party. Between these extremes there was a multitude of legal, semi-legal or illegal groups to choose from, but the concept of legality fluctuated. Most of the demonstrations were technically illegal, but not *as* illegal as, for instance, taking up arms for the New People's Army.

The armed struggle was, we were told, the highest way to serve the people. But if you disagreed with that, or if you were simply squeamish, there was plenty more to do. You might not fire the gun, but you might give shelter to the sick and wounded. Your home might become a venue for furtive meetings. You might distribute the Party paper, or pledge a monthly sum of money to the cause. Or – and this was typical of the times – you might be part of a group with a quite distinct purpose (human rights, for instance, or rural development) which nevertheless had its links with the underground. Unknown to you, one of its officers might be a Party member, and might be manipulating its work for Party purposes. So it was even possible to be a part of the underground without knowing it, and certainly to be one without admitting it to yourself.

The underground was a state of mind. You had shared enemies – the police, the military, the politicians, the American imperialists. You had a shared language, a kind of democratic slang, which dropped the polite forms of address. You could tell at once from the political jargon where a person's sympathies lay, and you could sometimes tell just from his clothes. Leather sandals, a tribal bracelet or belt, a native backpack from Mountain Province, a kerchief from Mindanao – but, if you could afford them, Levis.

People spoke, or rather sang, of going to the *bundok* – to the mountains, as the moment of joining the revolutionary struggle. But for most of us it was not like that. There was no definitive break from family and friends. We went on drinking beer, when we could afford it, and listening to western pop. The motto was 'Simple life, hard struggle', but that didn't stand in the way of an occasional trip to a night-club, or even a 'sauna'. We tended to drop out of college because, we said, more could be learned on the streets. But from time to time we did go to the mountains for what we called Exposure.

Exposure might last for anything from a week to a lifetime. It was a way of testing your commitment. If your Collective thought you might have doubts about the Cause, they would start to exert gentle pressure to get you to go for Exposure. See for yourself, they would say, how the comrades live, how total their commitment is, how undivided, how unquestioning. And because commitment was the magic word, the goal, the ideal, your first Exposure would be a great moment in your life.

It didn't work for me. At the end of 1986 I went north from Manila to the Sierra Madre to spend ten days at a guerrilla camp. Marcos had been overthrown earlier that year and the Aquino government had negotiated a limited truce with the Communists. The confidence of the underground was high. Prominent members had surfaced in Manila and had appeared on the streets and on television. The people's struggle was getting as much publicity as it could wish for.

Our guide to the camp was a fourteen-year-old girl, pretty and innocent-looking, and with a pistol tucked into her waistband. Wherever we went, we kept meeting these juvenile soldiers – the youngest was twelve years old – and although there were also middle-aged cadres there seemed to be an age gap. There was a shortage of recruits in their twenties, people of my age. I wondered what had happened to them.

When we talked to the children they gave us identical answers about what they were doing and why. We would ask them, Are you ready to die for the revolution? And they would reply sincerely that they were. They had already taken part in ambushes.

We would ask them, Are you ready to kill? And they would say Yes, to serve the People. I couldn't begin to say so to my companions, or to my friends in Manila, but what I really thought was: these children should be back in school, the revolution has robbed them of their childhood. What was more, I thought the barrios would be better off without the NPA. They had been poor before, but at least they had not been living in fear. Now to think all that was to contemplate the unthinkable – to doubt the correctness of the people's war, not to believe in the organisation of youth when my own work was supposed to be in the organisation of youth. As we parted, our teenage guide said, 'Next time you come, we may not be here any more. Remember, we are in a war.' She seemed to have been conditioned to accept that she was going to die.

For a while the truce continued, and I continued with my work. By now I had met Kazuo and he offered to lend me his video camera. A group of peasants had come to Manila and were camped outside the Ministry of Agrarian Reform. I thought a documentary could be made about their campaign, and I applied to my group for funds. For a week I filmed them night and day, all their meetings, everything that happened in the camp. On the last day there was to be a march.

On any large demonstration in those days, provision was made for security. A routine would be rehearsed, a cordon of linked arms, ready for confrontation with the police or military, to prevent people being snatched and beaten up. A standard operational procedure had been worked out by those higher up. There was a buddy system. You must know the person on your right and on your left, the guy in front and the guy behind. The aim was to avoid infiltration by military agents.

Before the march, I filmed the exercises of the security group. Most of them were from an urban youth group, very militant. They had sticks and stones and were ready for a fight. The plan was to march to Malacanang Palace and demand audience with President Aquino, and by the time the demonstrators reached the centre of town they were in an aggressive mood.

I detached myself from the main group and went ahead to Malacanang. The approach to the palace begins at Mendiola Bridge, whose barbed wire had been symbolically dismantled during the February Revolution. I was shocked to see that the defences were all back in place. The police were officially unarmed, but the military, in the ranks behind them, were in full combat gear.

There was a truck parked behind the first row of police, and I took my place on it, together with the press. I felt nervous, as if behind enemy lines. I tried not to let the camera shake, as the procession approached. They were singing a song from the war of independence, a song about the death of a hero. Jimmy Tadeo, the leader of the farmers' union, was in front with his negotiating team, and they at once began arguing with the police to let them through, but while this was happening a scuffle broke out at the other end of the line. I panned to the right. Stones were flying, and the police were beating up the crowd.

A few moments later there came a great burst of gunfire. At once the photographers jumped from the truck and ran toward the action. As the firing continued, the camera seemed to leap in my hand. I panned desperately left and right, seeking out what was going on. I zoomed out. The crowd was running away and bodies lay on the ground. The soldiers seemed confused, panicked even, firing their armalites into the air. An officer was pacing to and fro, drawing heavily on a cigarette. I zoomed in again on one of the bodies. The photographers had rushed forward, and some of them were helping to drag the man away. By now they were the only people on the intersection, moving among the dead and wounded. On the sidestreet people were weeping and shrieking curses at the military. Still there were occasional gunshots.

I took my eye from the viewfinder and looked around me. I was alone on the truck and had been in the middle of the firing. I climbed down quickly to the side of the bridge, where a man was being beaten up by plainclothes police, covering his bleeding head and pleading, 'Please, please, I am not with them. I am for Cory. I am for Cory.' I rejoined the press, who were busy loading the wounded and dead onto jeepneys. The streets had cleared, leaving a debris of newspapers, streamers, slippers, shoes, blood and brains.

A policeman grabbed me by the arm. 'You filmed the lot, didn't you?' 'No, I've just arrived,' I said. He made as if to take the camera, but a friend intervened. We jumped into a jeepney and made our way towards the Bonifacio Monument, through the darkening, deserted streets. Here some of the demonstrators had regrouped, but the mounted police had them trapped on both sides. Plainclothesmen with armalites and white headbands were firing into the air and the crowd was mercilessly tear-gassed. Finally, they lay on the ground to surrender.

It was the end of the truce. As soon as news broke of the Mendiola massacre, the guerrilla negotiators disappeared underground. Their presence in the capital, their appearances on television and at demonstrations, their open propagandising had intensely provoked the Right, and the massacre was their way of getting back at them. The faint hope of a negotiated peace was finished, and the Left blamed Cory.

A couple of weeks later, in the editing studio, I had a moment of real terror, like a delayed shock, when I viewed my footage for the first time. The police had been claiming that they were unarmed in the demonstration, but the plainclothesmen in my footage clearly had guns. I felt like a witness in danger.

But there was another feeling that crept up on me during the editing of the documentary. Because my group had raised the money for the tapes, it was considered that the film did not belong to me. The editing, and the script, passed into other hands. There had to be consultations. Somewhere in the background, at one remove, the Party line was being injected into the film. The peasants had to look like ordinary farmers with legitimate grievances, so a scene in which one of them was shown drawing a large hammer and sickle in chalk on the road was dropped. Jimmy Tadeo had to be shown in a good light, so a scene in which he treated the Minister like a child was also omitted. Care was taken to tone down the provocative moments of the crowd. I watched all this happening, and wrote in my diary: 'Someday, I am going to resign.'

I was at that stage a candidate member of the Communist Party, but I already knew that if they offered me full membership I would not accept it. I couldn't take the responsibility, and I couldn't live under their discipline. If I was to make a film again, I would have to do it independently or with people who knew about film itself, not propagandists.

The Mendiola massacre was my first experience

of violent death, and it affected me strangely. I didn't find myself weeping over the corpses. I was much more affected by the families' grief at the funeral. The peasants had had their legitimate grievances, and had the right to demonstrate and not be killed for it. But behind these mass actions there was an unseen hand moving: that of the Party in its bid for power. The Party was never frank about this, except with those close to it. I didn't like the way people were being manipulated.

But I kept my feelings to myself. I guessed that an offer of full party membership was not far off, and that it would be a moment of truth for me. In the meantime I got a different offer, the chance to study for a year in Japan. I accepted with a show of coolness: I had never been abroad before, and was unprepared for the experience of being projected straight into another country. But at the same time it was a great relief to slip away from the Movement, to take a break, after six years of it.

I arrived in Japan just at the time of the flower-viewing festival. Exactly a year later I became fully initiated into a new underground, the colony we Filipinos are building in Japan.

10

Filipino Sunday

ON SUNDAY MORNING, Kotobuki looks like what it is – home to the dregs of Japanese society. Among the litter, the coffee cans and chopsticks, the vomit and urine, it's not unusual to find a day-labourer lying in the street beside his empty sake bottle. Some of the bars never close, and a day's drinking might begin at seven, indoors or out – in the Korean-run bar, or on the street by the open braziers. It's a rough place – the mention of Koto is enough to make your Japanese friends alarmed – but it has some merits. This is the part of Japan where I can greet an old man on the street and be greeted in return. Koto scares the Japanese, but it's the only place where I'm not scared.

It's a question of territory: Koto belongs to a series of overlapping groups. Korean Japanese-run small shops and bars and a few cheap inns. We Filipinos provide the illegal workforce, and although there may be a few individual Pakistanis or Latinos, if a Pakistani group tried to form, we'd see them off. The communists have a base here as well, with their labour unions, and the surprising thing is that this is the only place where I have not seen them clash with the Yakuza.

The Yakuza themselves – the subordinates, that is, not the oyabun – will be around on Sunday, keeping an eye on things: the betting shops, the pachinko parlours, the snack bars. They're in their casual clothes, and they're amused at the way we always get dressed up on Sundays. They call out to ask where we're going. Church? Oh yes, they say, you're Christians, aren't you. That's why. And then they make the sign of the cross, or try to. They must have picked that up from mafia films.

'We're going to church,' we say, 'to ask God's blessing, so we don't get arrested.' And we make the handcuff sign, placing our wrists together at an angle.

'There are police over there,' they say, pointing to the box.

'Don't worry,' we reply, unimpressed, 'they're our friends.' We know 'how to ride' the Yakuza, we say to ourselves; we know 'where to tickle' them. They're not our friends, exactly, but there is a coincidence of interest. Sometimes Filipinos will do errands for them, in the crack business for instance or as number runners. I knew one man who got so close to the Yakuza that he used to copy their look, with crinkly hair and dark glasses, but I never heard of a Filipino actually joining up. Nor did I ever hear of trouble between us and the Yakuzas in Koto. But there was a price for this. If we were shortchanged by their associates on our wages, we never complained, and, when we joked with them on the streets, we knew just how far we could go.

I always walked to church, but some people went by taxi. They liked to be sure that they would arrive spick and span, and they liked perhaps to give the impression that they weren't illegals. The advantage of walking on Sundays was that the pavements were strewn with *gomi* – TVs, Hi-Fis, rice-cookers, porno mags. Obviously you wouldn't arrive at church with a rice-cooker under your arm or your pockets stuffed with porn, but you most definitely would make a mental note of any interesting gomi, and even perhaps hide it or obscure it from other scavengers (those Russian seamen, for instance) till after the service.

The church is a twenty minute walk away, and that's the farthest we dare to go outside of Koto. It stands on a hill overlooking the port of Yokohama, and at the foot of the hill lies another Sunday rendez-vous, McDonalds. Hamburgers first, then Holy Com-munion. This particular McDonalds had a certain amorous character. Lovers – for instance Filipinas with Japanese husbands and a compatriot boyfriend on the side – would meet there before mass. Bar-girls and maids with *novios* from the Koto underground would spend their time off there. It was said that a raid on the church and on that McDonalds any Sunday morning would be guaranteed to yield a good catch. But neither place was ever investigated in my time.

The church, the Sacred Heart Cathedral, stands in the Yamate district, a wealthy area of foreign-occupied bungalows, and the congregation at the English language service is two-thirds Westerners – Americans and Europeans – one-third Filipino, and because I was in the habit of turning up late I often had to stand. Indeed sometimes I could hardly get in.

I used to arrive late because to me the service was more important for social than for spiritual reasons. That wasn't true of most of the community. Most people – even the worst of the bully boys – had their own prayer books and sacred images, their gold crosses and religious texts carefully copied out by hand and stuck on the walls of their rooms. They kept their Bibles either beside the bed or displayed in some prominent place, and the kind of Bibles they had were annotated by topic, so that you could look up a subject such as 'confidence' or 'safety'. You would never place a Bible alongside other books on a shelf, or beneath anything at all. You might share a Bible but you would never lend it. If there was a fire, it would be the first thing you would try to rescue. If you lost your Bible, that would be a very bad omen, and it would be bad luck to be separated from it –

for instance, by being put under arrest. But in that case, at least, you would always have your prayer book – wherever you were, you would always have in your pocket some money, a loved one's photo, a list of telephone numbers, a prayer book and – in the case of most men – a knife.

And what we had said to the Yakuza was true: most of us went to church in order to pray not to be arrested. Whatever their sins, my friends thought that if they had taken communion they would be safer from the police. Church gave them confidence and a kind of relief from the tensions of hiding. And this was the moment in the week dedicated to remembering our friends and family back home.

That was the spiritual side – and it was intensely felt. But church-going was also the centre of our weekly social life, and one of the chief attractions was the opportunity to see some beautiful girls. This was the first subject my friends and I would discuss on coming out of church, and as we stood around outside watching the congregation coming down the steps we would be on the look-out for an opportunity to approach them. Often the bullies would get in first, and it was important not to assume that a girl was unaccompanied in case you gave offence.

Even inside the church, a man could give offence. If he was an outsider, a stranger to Koto, and if he was dressed up in a suit (which is for us a pretentious way for a young man to dress) and wore a lot of gold, he would already be marked down as arrogant, and the bullies would wait for him outside the church. There they would engage him in conversation, and if he spoke to them in the wrong tone of voice, they would teach him a lesson, in front of everyone else. It would all happen very quickly – a slap in the face, a punch in the stomach, a public humiliation. And if he tried to do anything further about it he would be in big trouble.

This swiftness to take offence at a stranger's behaviour is known as a *kursonada*, a 'liking'. Used of a man and a girl, it means that the man has taken a fancy to the girl. Used of a man and a man, it always has the opposite, aggressive meaning. Someone has walked on to your patch. He has to be reminded he's a visitor. He has to pay his respects, just as a newcomer in the forest must pray first to the spirits. The tough guys, the fearless ones, the gangsters demand a kind of tribute. Once you were known, once your presence in the community was accepted, you could wear what you wanted, and what people wore to church was always the best they had.

This connection between new clothes and churchgoing is very strong in the Philippines. If you get a new pair of Levis, or Reebok, or Adidas, you will want to 'bless' them first, which means wearing them first to church, particularly on a special date, birthday, first communion, Christmas Eve or New Year's Day. If you go to church in Yokohama you will want to display the fruits of your illegal labour: gold chains, bracelets, rings, leather jackets, signature clothes both real and fake.

We were limited in our status symbols. All the rest of the congregation would drive to church, but though we could easily have afforded cars we couldn't have completed the legal paperwork involved. Not one of us had a vehicle – not even a bicycle (which would need to be registered). There were abandoned bicycles everywhere in Koto, but they were no use to us without their papers – we would have been accused of robbery.

Much of what we wore to church came from the flea market in Odori Park – another important Sunday event. The older men from Koto would have got there before church, and would be boasting of their new acquisitions as they came out of the service. But they were the Odori Boys, the real connoisseurs, grandfathers mostly, with enough grandchildren back home to keep them busy buying second-hand clothes and toys. At the gemba, they would talk obsessively about the Odori market, which was held once a fortnight, and which was renowned among us for the most astonishing bargains.

The Odori Boys could never get used to the way the Japanese threw things out, the way things lost their value. Back home, we would find a use for everything. A family would never throw out, for instance, bottles or paper. Nor would it be given away for recycling. It would be sold to dealers in junk. There is no second-hand clothes market in the Philippines – a garment is passed from hand to hand until it ends up as a floorcloth or a doormat. No one would ever throw out a piece of cloth – it would feel like a sin. And so a flea market in which a pair of Levis could be bought for a few pounds or a shirt – 'a long sleeve' – for fifty pence was a most remarkable thing. And the rooms of the Odori Boys – most of our rooms – were piled with neat parcels of bargains awaiting shipment back home. And people built their own Hi-Fi systems, Odori style, which they yearned to play freely at full volume – which they *did* play, sometimes, and got themselves thrown out of the house, or out of the country, for making too much noise.

Odori Park, deserted normally, excepting for the few down-and-outs who went to drink there in the sun, or couples at evening on their way to the near-by love hotels, with its litter-strewn camellia hedges, its poplars rising out of the concrete and the regular rumbling of underground trains from beneath, was no great beauty spot. But it had a special place in our lives. The traders were all Japanese, the customers nearly all immigrants. We always came and went by the Kannai Station end, because there was a police box at the other. But the flea market itself was never raided. It seemed to be part of our permitted existence.

And that existence could be at its most melancholy on a Sunday, even if Sunday was the highlight of the week. This was the day you would wonder why you were in Japan, the day you would most miss your family and friends, when the focus of your mind would suddenly shift. This was the day for writing letters, or splashing out on a telephone call. Some people would spend a whole *lapad*, ten thousand yen or two days' net earnings, on a single call home, and they would do this once a week. A third of their savings for half an hour's conversation. We longed to know how to cheat the machine. There had been one booth in Tokyo where it was said you could get an overseas call at a local rate. Every local phone booth in Koto had been tested by our best men, but we never managed to outwit the system – unlike the coin laundries, stoves and vending machines. We were avid for letters, but often afraid to be traced by the authorities through the mail. So if you were receiving letters at your place of residence, you might use a pseudonym, which in this context meant anything other than your passport name, which itself was quite likely to be a fake. Thus my friend Manny used his real name as a pseudonym. Willy, on the other hand, borrowed the name of a Japanese co-worker, gave it the wrong honorific and had his letters sent to 'Yoshida-san'. Apart from the fact that this ruse made his letters look comical and odd to the Japanese eye, the use of false names put one to a certain extent at the mercy of the landlord or landlady of the building, who had to know exactly what your arrangements were, and who tended to withhold letters against payment of overdue rent.

The alternative to all this was the man we used to call the Father of Perpetual Help, Father Maurice, our postman and our priest, whose office had become a sanctuary for us every Sunday. A group of Japanese volunteers would cook, and you could eat well there, including Filipino dishes, for two hundred yen (as opposed to a thousand for a comparable meal outside). As soon as he arrived after mass, Father Maurice would take his place on the sofa in the corner and produce the good news, the pack of letters, from his pocket, teasing the recipients as he read out each name, with guesses as to the sender: Oh, lucky man, here is a letter from your loving wife, your girlfriend . . . see, she's always thinking of you, you should be more industrious . . .

And the recipients, if they were in a mood to boast, would read out the more loving passages to the rest of us, and we would look up from our cards or mahjong and cluck our tongues, saying, 'Yes, your wife loves you so much, maybe she's pregnant again,' (the kind of jocular remark which is either taken in good part or lands you up with broken limbs). Many people, especially the younger workers, were worried about their wives' fidelity. They had left them, as they put it, 'guarded' – their mothers, grandmothers and trusted relatives around the barrio having been instructed to keep an eye on them. Meanwhile they consoled themselves with the thought that they had the economic advantage – it was their wives who had everything to lose. Unlike husbands in the Philippines, who would normally hand over the whole wage packet to their wives and receive back an allowance, migrant workers sometimes remitted money to their own accounts and kept their wives on an allowance so that, just in case anything did go wrong, they would still have their nest-egg at the end. And in the meantime every married man I knew, apart from one old man, was unfaithful one way or another to his wife, and some of the wives knew this and understood it. And sometimes in their letters the wives made the rules explicit: the husband might have a girlfriend, but he must never have a child by her. That was the One Commandment.

But that understanding attitude only lasted as long as the benefits lasted, the remittances came and the money piled up in the bank, or the house was built or improved, or the mortgage paid. But when the advantages ceased the letters would turn bitter and the wives would beg their husbands to come home. And the husbands might be faced with the knowledge that they had got used to Koto, with their live-in companion, no family, no relatives, none of the restrictions of barrio life. They had become addicted to their exile. Unfree by the rules of Japan, they had nevertheless found freedom from their own morality and culture. This was the charm of Koto, the lure.

But many of these men were more than just husbands and fathers: they were heads of families; if not, in fact, they had become heads of families by virtue of becoming breadwinners. And so the letters would come from other family members asking for decisions on important issues – the sale or purchase of a piece of land, what course a child should study – or matters of detail, such as the style of furniture to be bought. And for every migrant worker with money in the bank, there were a dozen family members back home with ideas as to how the money should be spent, and dozens more neighbours with proposals for loans or bargain sales of property.

And so the money saved was burning a hole in dozens of different pockets, and the letters would be full of schemes and get-rich-quick wheezes: plans to found beauty parlours, dance studios, recruitment agencies for Japan, bureaus purporting to acquire US citizenship for their clients, speculations, opportunities to snap up foreclosed properties, unique chances to bank-roll small-scale treasure-hunting initiatives, illegal logging ventures and gold-prospecting in Mountain Province.

The letters were our lifeblood – we needed them whether or not they were going to cheer us up with their news and their demands. And we needed to send them, even though this was sometimes extremely awkward to arrange, because we might be working in the docklands, far from a post office. Sometimes my friends and I arranged that one of us would take a day's *yasumi*, or leave, just to post letters, rather than take the risk of leaving the worksite during the lunch-break. On such days, people would also take the opportunity to make their remittances home, and I was always surprised at how easy it was to do this.

The letters, written on Sunday afternoons, were full of the melancholy of the day: complaints about the weather (which were true) and about the irregularity of work (which were not necessarily true, but which maintained a degree of privacy around the subject, i.e. how much the writer was earning); then came the advice, the delegation of authority and, most importantly in any married man's letter, the issues surrounding the rearing of the children.

For, generally speaking, people missed their children more than they missed their wives. They talked more about them at the gemba, showing their pictures around, and their letters. The children's letters were the most cheering part of any package from home, and if a man opened his wallet it was normally the children's photographs that were most prominently displayed. If a man phoned home, it was with the children that he would spend most time talking. And I once witnessed the homecoming of a friend from Japan – a surprise arrival since the man had been ill

– and was struck by the way he embraced his son for several minutes before turning to his wife and saying, 'Hey, where's my kiss?'

Our Sunday meetings at Father Maurice's – in which the letters were handed out, we ate, and people whiled away the rest of the day – were the scene of several informal discussions as to whether we should found some form of self-help organisation. There were several non-Filipino groups administering to our needs: the church, both Protestant and Catholic, catered for women in distress, provided us with the venue for our meetings, and gave us informal advice of both a spiritual and practical kind. The labour union and the Communists offered legal services, political education and acted as intermediary in cases where a worker had a serious complaint against an employer. They campaigned for the legislation of foreign labour in Japan, organising symposia and film shows, getting the issue into the papers.

We had nothing of our own, in the formal sense. Informally, the groupings that had sprung up were based either on religion or on province of origin. We had gangs, but no union, and we were prevented, being illegals, from joining the Japanese labour union. The Communists were always telling us that we ought to organise, pointing out among other things that it would enable them to help us more easily if there was one representative organisation which could put forward a set of demands or requests.

But we were dubious. Nobody was talking in very ambitious terms: there was no question of strikes or wage negotiations or a code of practice on work conditions or hours worked. Our illegal status precluded any of that. But there were practical problems encountered every day: people needed help leaving the country after they had been arrested – a ticket had to be bought and their belongings had to be got together; when quarrels arose among ourselves, there was no mediating body; there was no way of sharing out available work during times of scarcity; when there were medical problems, we always had to go to outside organisations.

What people feared was that if we started an organisation to deal with such matters, we would give the authorities one more reason to arrest us. We would be associating ourselves with the Communists, with the anti-government forces. And although the Japanese Communists were legal, we associated them with our Communists back home – to our way of thinking they were illegal and subversive. They were vociferous in defence of our struggle, they were promoting it. They knew more about it than we did. We suspected them of harbouring a hidden agenda. And they would invite us to meetings at which they showed us film shows and slides of our own country, and they thought this good political education. But we sat there ashamed, because they were showing us poverty and ugliness, whereas we thought we had a beautiful country. My friends would say, 'If they go on showing this kind of film, people will look down on Filipinos even more.'

Nevertheless, we did think that an association was a good idea, and over a series of Sunday meetings we set it up, drew up a rule-book, elected officers and gathered subscriptions. Father Maurice took charge of the funds, but that didn't prevent a certain amount of cynicism among the community about the way the funds were spent. To an extent, these doubts were justified, nevertheless over its first few months the association did manage to address the kind of problems we had envisaged: it helped people with health problems, it procured air tickets for deportees and gave token donations, it mediated in quarrels between warring gangs, it organised a special Mass to be held in Filipino.

The President was one of the *Tiradores*, the Muntinlupa gang, who called themselves Intruders in Japan. He was tough – he thought nothing of going to some Yokohama club and picking a fight with a couple of black Americans over some Japanese girl. But he was respected and not only for his strength. (I saw the face of the man who had been messing with his girlfriend – he had lost four front teeth.) He was intensely Filipino, unable to speak English, uninterested in doing so, and with hardly any Japanese to get by on. He provided something of a contrast with the Vice-President of the Association, who always addressed meetings in English, and claimed to be a qualified lawyer. (He was the son of a judge, and had flunked his exams.)

The Vice-President, who had confidently expected to win the presidency on the first ballot, stood on his dignity, addressing the President in his not-too-perfect English. The President countered this by bringing along an interpreter to their meetings. He was a good president, but in the end he did something slightly strange: he announced his impending departure home, and the Communists held a farewell party in his honour. But a short while later he was back in Koto as a Standing Man. For some reason or other he had decided to go underground – a deeper underground than the one we all shared.

11

The Missionary

EVERY MORNING DODONG would wake me up with a soft tap at the steel door – always the same one-two rhythm. One day his alarm failed, and when the knock came it sounded different – softer, as if shy, perhaps the tapping of fingernails rather than the knuckle. I reached out from my bed and turned the knob. A small, dark, fugitive face, like a cat in a kitchen, sneaked in. It was a girl just younger than myself.

The first time I saw her had been in church. She was dressed all in black: black veil, blouse, belt, skirt, stockings, shoes and gloves, as if in the deepest mourning. At the end of mass, she stood at the door and handed out red roses. She had looked elegant and rich. Later, I had often seen her with an expensive bouquet, or sometimes with a stuffed panda or bear.

The previous day I had met her, talking animatedly with the Standing Men. She introduced herself, surprisingly and rather formally, in Japanese. She called herself Danny. Whenever anyone asked her name, be it a Filipino or a Japanese, she was always formal. She spoke good Japanese, to the delight of the Oji-chans, whom she addressed in the manner of a granddaughter, before elegantly asking them for a hundred yen for the coffee machine.

This time, in her long white T-shirt and no bra, she looked a waif. She was weird, but I was attracted to her humour, although slightly less attracted when, just as I was boarding the work-bus, she requested a loan of ten thousand. She was on her way to Tokyo, she had money there, she would pay me back . . . I lent her four.

Danny was considered a bad omen in Kotobuki. Because of her, the men said, we would be in trouble. Everybody knew her, and they knew her as small, dark, ugly, talkative (they called her 'Takatak'), a fool and Romero's one-night stand. At worst, the Filipinos suspected she might be an immigration or police spy. But the Oji-chans thought of her as a plain Japayuki-san in search of a quick yen. All the men routinely asked her to their rooms.

Now, unasked, she was in my room.

'Can I come in?' she said meekly. She was clutching a yellow bag, and a bright coloured sweater was draped around her shoulders.

'Come in quickly,' I said. 'You might be seen by the neighbours.

'We've just come from a disco with the President,' she said, slumping onto the futon. 'I haven't even had an hour of sleep.'

I began to clear up the other futon.

'Books, magazines, and a dictionary!' she exclaimed, as if she had seen a snake.

'They're not mine,' I lied. 'They're a friend's.'

'And a typewriter!' She saw another serpent.

One by one she went through my possessions, asking what everything was. I hadn't even wanted her to know my full name, but she found it on a folder of poems, which she riffled through. Then she raised her palm towards me. 'Give me five, man.'

I returned the gesture twice. Then, to distract her from further enquiries I told her to get some sleep on the futon. She turned away from me and curled up like a child.

I went down the corridor, washed and changed my clothes, ashamed to do so in front of her, although I'm sure she wouldn't have minded.

On my return to the room I found her reading the poems. 'If you can't get work,' she said, 'let's go to Tokyo.'

'I have to get a job today,' I said. 'I've no money at all.'

'Oh, here's your money,' she said, producing a ¥10,000 note. 'You can have it all if you don't have anything.'

'No,' I said, 'I still have money for lunch, but if

you don't mind I'll just get back the four thousand you owe me.' She reached again into the bag. Clearly she was back in funds, but I didn't want to take advantage.

If I'd been a Visayan, like her, there would have been nothing odd about her coming to my room, and we would have spoken freely in a shared dialect. But because we were not province-mates, her familiarity was strange. I left her with instructions not to go through my papers.

On the street, I met Wilson and told him about my visitor. 'Did you sleep with her last night?' he said immediately.

I knew I was going to be teased. 'No, she knocked on my door at five.'

'If you don't get a ride today, ride her.'

That was our expression when there was no work. If you can't get a ride on the bus, ride your futon, ride your girl – if you have one. And indeed most of us didn't get a job that day. Even the sacho-of-last-resort, the SLR, didn't take a single Filipino. We would have to rot on our futons.

Then Danny appeared on the corner. Paong, a well-known joker, called her over. 'I'll introduce you to a handsome gentleman,' he said. We waited in amused anticipation.

'Which handsome gentleman?' said Danny, looking from face to face with a regal manner, inspecting us all. She knew the game that was about to begin.

'That handsome guy over there,' said Paong, pointing to Boy Puki (Boy 'Cunt', an obsessive sexual boaster). Boy was indeed handsome, but he happened to have a beautiful girlfriend, and he happened to despise Danny for her looks.

'If you bring her over here,' said Boy Cunt, 'I'll spit in her face. I'll spit in her face.'

'OK,' said Paong to Danny, 'I'll introduce you to a *tall*, handsome gentleman.' He approached Romero, the Fashion Model, Danny's former lover.

'I'll bet you a lapad you can't get her to come near me,' said Romero. He had kicked Danny out when another of his girlfriends had turned up, and he assumed that she wouldn't have the face to confront him.

'OK,' said Paong, 'it's a bet.'

He approached Danny again. 'That tall guy in green,' he said, 'he wants to talk to you.'

'And who would he be – this handsome guy in green?' Her voice took on a note of contempt. 'I see, I see,' she said, and crossed the road and went straight up to Romero. He stepped aside, but it was too late. The crowd booed and jeered at him.

'I won,' said Paong. 'Where's the money?'

Romero had to save face. 'One more time,' he said. 'Let her come near me.'

Paong called her again, and again she consented. They met like David and Goliath, Danny being only half Romero's height. To the cheers of the crowd,

Danny looked up at his face, defiantly. Romero half turned away, embarrassed. It was a daring and unusual act for a woman, and very shaming to the man. I thought he was going to slap her, which would have been even more shaming to him.

'Oh, *that's* the one, is it?' said Danny, turning slowly from Romero to face the crowd, her features twisting as she delivered the line she always used about him in her bitterness: '*I don't like men who lick like puppies.*'

This time nobody laughed. To do so would have been to ask for a fight with Romero, who stood there dumbstruck with humiliation. That *he*, the Fashion Model, should be revealed as so undiscriminating. To have gone with Danny! To have *licked* Danny!

Unlike the other women of Koto, Danny was well educated. She came from a modest family of farmers in Leyte, but she had been brought up in Manila by a maiden aunt who had sent her to an exclusive women's university. Her upbringing had been strict, and she had no boyfriends in Manila. Another aunt, who had married a Japanese, brought her over to Tokyo as a babysitter, and for a year she had studied Nihonggo, in which she was fluent.

Her aunt's idea in sending her to school had been two-fold: to enable her to talk to the child she was bringing up, and to improve her marriageability. There was an old man, a family friend, who was considered a suitable match and who came regularly to the house, bearing gifts for Danny. But Danny rebelled: whether for the obvious natural reasons, or because she was already beginning to go crazy, she refused to play the submissive role expected of a poor relation. She was not going to be married off, and her way of avoiding that fate showed a degree of reckless courage.

She had discovered that her aunt, in common with many women in her position in Japan, had a Filipino lover on the side. (This was one of the activities in which Koto excelled: it was a great provider of romance for bored, lonely Filipina brides. The president of our association was a specialist in this kind of service, who later became involved with this same aunt.) Now Danny threatened that if she was pushed any further towards marriage, she would reveal all. The aunt's response was an outburst of physical violence so strong that it left Danny hospitalised for several days. She left home and was taken into care by an organisation that helped women in distress.

At this point Danny's position in Japan was not hopeless. She had language skills, a legal identity, and connections – everything an illegal worker might aspire to. I do not know what drew her initially to the world of Kotobuki. Life was hard, but there was a kind of freedom, and a sense of community among the illegals. We lacked what we would have relied on back home – the support of our extended families in times of need. But this general absence of family turned the whole community into a family – a strange family, but Danny's tragedy was that her strangeness didn't fit in with ours. A part of her seemed too respectable to belong to Tokyo rather than Koto. The other side was not respectable at all.

We all assumed that, when she disappeared for a while, she was on the job. That alone would have made her no different from any number of women in Koto, each of whom might have the right to a certain kind of respect. For Danny, her descent into the underworld represented a humiliation. She courted it and she came to suffer from it more and more.

The first thing that happened was that she lost her grip on the respectable side of her life. I came to understand some of this when she invited Akihiro and me to accompany her to Tokyo. She said, 'Don't dress casually. Please be formal. My friends are not ordinary people.' But when we picked her up on the day she was wearing a cheap nightdress and wooden sandals. Naturally everyone stared at her in the train. She had no bra, and a nipple was protruding like the teat of a Babyflo. We had to pay for her ticket, she said she'd lost her bank passbook.

She had said that she would show us her room in Tokyo and introduce us to her friends. She would lend me books. She had spoken of the grandness of the area she lived in, and it was indeed grand. The houses were modern, with luxurious gardens full of bright flowers and well-fed dogs. Even Akihiro was in awe of the wealth. It was the sort of place where foreign families would live with their Filipina maids. It had a decidely Western feel.

It was a weekday morning. Not many people were about, and I was glad. Akihiro and I tried to dissociate ourselves from Danny, as she clattered along the street in her nightdress and clogs. She was a most improbable resident of the area.

She unlatched a front gate. 'Do you live *here*?' I said. She put a finger to her lips. 'Don't make too much noise. Wait for me here in the garden.' She went up to the house and, avoiding the front door, made her way down into what seemed a basement. We stood around awkwardly, already regretting the trip, hoping that no one would come out and see us, trying not to be mistaken for thieves. After a few minutes Danny called us to help her with her things.

We found ourselves in an unlit garage. Danny's possessions were packed in half a dozen cardboard boxes and assorted tins and bags. She was rummaging through them, looking for her passbook, which I immediately realised did not exist. To contain my embarrassment I pretended to help. Neither Akihiro nor I knew what to say: Danny had certainly misled us, but she didn't seem to think she had.

A woman called out in a kind, restrained voice, 'Danny, we've moved your stuff.' It was an American in her late forties. She had appeared at a door that gave into the house.

'Mummy Esther,' said Danny, 'these are my friends.'

The woman acknowledged us with a faint smile. 'Danny,' she said, 'have you found a room yet?'

Danny told some story about a friend who was about to vacate some lodgings.

The woman, who was the wife of a Protestant minister, went on to say that she needed the room immediately for her daughter, so Danny should take her remaining things as soon as possible. She said this politely, but with an unmistakeable sharpness. Then she disappeared.

By now, Akihiro and I were hungry, embarrassed and not a little angry. 'Here are my books,' said Danny, appeasingly and with a touch of pride, 'you can choose any of them.' The box contained a few Mills and Boons and a Bible. I was trying to think how to get away from Danny. She had stopped her aimless rummaging and was just standing there. She had run out of things to say and do.

In the garden, we started to say goodbye, telling her we had to go to Akihiro's office. Hurriedly, she said she would walk with us. Equally hurriedly, we said that was not necessary. We went to a park and sat there for a while. We drank water from a tap to stave off our hunger. Finally, as we broke away, Danny said, 'Can you lend me some money?' I gave her some, and we left her alone on the swing. From a distance, she looked like a child.

She came to my room like a thief in the night. Sometimes she was in tatters, sometimes in the expensive black gear she had worn in church. She slept in her clothes, and I never touched her, but the men teased me mercilessly nevertheless. Finally I used the landlord as an alibi to get rid of her.

Now her behaviour became even stranger. She appeared on the street corner and made a speech to the Standing Men. 'I did not come here,' she began, pointing to the sky, 'to put myself on a pedestal, to be gazed at, honoured or admired. I came here to live with you – you who are discriminated against and looked down upon by this society.' The men gathered round, laughing and cheering.

She went on, 'I want to help the president of the association. He's in difficulty. Imagine, he is sacrificing himself for the association, and for the good of all Filipinos here. But he can only do so much. He's an illegal, and cannot openly come out to organise and solicit help.

'I know the consul general of the Philippines embassy. I can talk to her personally. She's the only human there. Most of the staff are croco-diles. If you can only get organised and everyone cooperates, we can ask the help of the embassy.'

One of the men shouted, 'Yehey! Let's vote Takatak for mayor. Takatak for mayor of Koto!'

In fact she had done a disservice to the president. He had come back late one night with his girlfriend to find Danny alone in their room, dancing with the stereo on at full volume. The next day they were kicked out.

'Why did you do that, Danny?' I asked.

'I did it on purpose.'

'So what did you get out of it?'

'I wanted people to hate me. The more they hate me, the happier I am!'

She often went on about Romero: 'He was like a hungry dog. He licked every part of my body to satisfy his thirst for the flesh. Even during my period. He sucked and drained my breasts. That's why they look so small now. Even my soul – he wanted to suck my soul.

'Who says he's handsome? How can a thin and blind . . . ' (Romero wore glasses) ' . . . homosexual be handsome. Come on, tell me. Maybe he's handsome for you, because he dresses neatly, like a fashion model. But I tell you, people who are so clean that not a speck can be found in their rooms – these people are hiding an excessive dirt. These people are dangerous.

'And remember,' her voice reached a climax of sarcasm, 'they are the kind of people who go to church every Sunday. They confess their sins and receive holy communion. How dare they!'

'I will not leave Kotobuki,' she said, 'until I fulfil my mission.'

'And may I know what your mission is?'

'Now is not the time to reveal it. You will know some time. Just wait for events to happen. You will see.'

I found her one morning outside our building, Bible in hand. She was furiously underlining passages with a red felt marker. She offered to teach one of the girls to read the Bible. First she turned the radio to disco music. Then she turned the volume up full. Then she started reading at the top of her voice. Not even God could have understood what she was reading.

Finally, nobody accepted her any more. She had begun as a bird of ill omen. Then she became a serious liability. She was continually talking on the streets, even when the police were passing. We were all trying to live invisibly. Knowing this full well, she would do the opposite. People were scared she would give the police reason to raid our rooms.

Her mission had been to help, and the last object of her attention was a prostitute called Jinky, who had become pregnant. Jinky's live-in partner, Randy, used to beat her up almost every day, and she often came to my room to hide. Danny spent hours with Jinky, caressing her womb and talking to the foetus. 'When you grow up,' she would say, 'don't be like your father. Don't become a sadist.'

And Jinky, who had left one sadistic Japanese husband only to find herself in the same plight, would join in, 'You stand up for me. You get revenge for me.'

Eventually Randy put an end to all this with a threat of rape. He said to Danny, 'Don't come here any more, because once I get an erection you'll be in trouble.'

Danny's response was defiant mockery. 'Come on,' she said, withdrawing her hands for a moment from Jinky's womb, 'don't waste time. I dare you.'

I left them together and went up to my room. From the window, I could see Danny walking toward the station, lugging the bag which contained all her paraphernalia. She called that bag her house. Once again she was moving on, and she looked deeply forsaken, like a daughter in disgrace with the whole community.

12

Scissors, Paper, Stone

WILSON'S ROOM WAS as neat as Wilson. Of all my friends, he was the only one who always ironed his clothes, which he kept neatly stacked in a drawer. And his acquisitions, piled up on shelves, told of his interests in life: the flea market souvenirs, the porno collection picked up off the street, the Bible he read every night.

When we wanted to tease him, we called him Mamma's Boy. He had lived a cossetted life back home, graduating in civil engineering and taking a government job before giving up everything for Japan. He had come through immigration dressed as a businessman, but now the suit was folded away in the attaché-case. He had taken well to a day-labourer's life, but he still preserved the orderly comforts of home. In his stories he often referred to his mother, and his savings lay in her bank account. A large stuffed teddy-bear in the corner was reserved for the girlfriend waiting in his home province.

He had three current girlfriends. The one back home, to whom he sent money on request, was his college sweetheart. The one in Bahrain had made of him a Praise-the-Lord Christian: he read the Bible every night, said grace before eating and was regular in Sunday attendance. The third girlfriend was for Saturday nights: he would regularly visit the bar where she worked and was trying to inveigle her out. All the correspondence with these girls (and he received letters almost every day, addressed to a Japanese pseudonym known to the mama-san) was kept in a neat pile, and there was a collage of their photographs in a large frame on the wall.

'When was the last time you slept with a girl?' I asked him.

'Almost a year ago now. How about you?'

'I'm a bit luckier. Just before I came here, many moons ago.'

'How much did you pay?'

'Not much. A few hundred pesos.'

'Me,' said Wilson, 'I spent five lapad, two weeks' savings. It was my first month in Japan, and I was so obsessed with that Pinay.' She had priced herself like a Japanese, as they all did. There were no special rates for Filipinos.

But there was a possibility of cheap sex, and the sacho-of-last-resort pointed it out to us on the way to work. 'If you want to have *sok-sok*,' he said, stopping at the red light, 'the place is here. That one is three thousand. That one's eight thousand.'

'What's three thousand,' I asked.

'Three thousand is *jangkenpo*,' he said, making the scissors sign, 'and eight thousand is sok-sok.'

Sok-sok, a Filipino word, he illustrated with the Spanish fig. Jangkenpo was the same scissors-paper-stone game we used back home to decide who would be 'it' in hide-and-seek.

One lapad, ten thousand, would cover us for a day out at Jangkenpo. We discussed the matter for days, the main question being would we join in, or would we just watch? We didn't know exactly what the deal would be – public or private. I'd seen a live show with Kazuo, on the back streets of Tokyo. They are strictly speaking illegal, and are occasionally raided. I thought it unlikely that the place we had been shown, which was on a main road, would offer a similar spectacle. But the live shows are all run by the Yakuza.

On the day we took a shower in the welfare building, before going to Wilson's room, where he carefully trimmed his moustache and applied hair tonic and cologne. He wore a gold ring and a chain, his gold-plated watch and the leather shoes he had found at the flea market. He shook his hair and patted it, flicked the fluff from his shirt, picked up his key and his coin purse, and off we went.

We had a twenty minute walk ahead of us. My

belief was that it was better to stick to the sidestreets. Wilson had a theory that we'd be less noticeable among the crowds on the main streets, where there was anyway more space to run if the police tried to stop us. We argued this along the way, and unconsciously ended up taking a mixture of main and side street.

There was no name on the establishment, only a life-size cut-out of a sexy girl, hung from a post outside. We pushed through a scruffy curtain, down a narrow passage to the box-office. There were guards posted along the way, to give fair warning of a raid.

The foyer was undecorated, bare concrete walls dimly lit. On a wooden bench, a small girl in shorts was talking to the papa-san. Her feet were tucked up and she clasped her knees, and I knew from her accent that she was a Filipino. She glanced at us, then looked immediately away as if ashamed to be seen by her compatriots. The papa-san, fat and gangsterly, was old enough to be her grandfather. He seemed to be guarding the girl, stopping her from making a sudden dash for freedom.

Beyond another curtain lay the performing area – a catwalk leading to a small revolving stage. Coloured spotlights were the only concession to decor. The slow, high-pitched, melancholy music of the *enka* suggested that the taste being catered for was middle-aged or above. The audience was predominantly Japanese, the kind of men we worked alongside, and they looked like a congregation who were down on their luck: twenty starving souls.

We took our places on the second bench by the ramp. To our surprise there were two Filipinos in front of us – Bino and Ching. We'd come during working hours, at four o'clock, precisely to avoid meeting people we knew. We were a bit ashamed of the escapade. Bino and Ching had been there since the show opened, at eleven. We winked at each other.

The girls included two Koreans, a Taiwanese, a Colombian, two Japanese and the Filipina we had seen in the foyer. In the bleak, concrete sur-roundings, the colours of their long gowns shrieked under the spotlights. One by one they danced to an enka, as if the idea of dance were new to them, as if it were something they had heard of but never seen. There was a vague stretching of arms and a tentative repositioning of the feet. It was, as we say in Filipino, as if they were driving a very shy mosquito. The faces were hesitant, shy, unhappy, and it was a relief when western music was played and the Filipina came on, in short shorts and bra, to dispel some of the gloom. She knew how to dance, and she knew how to give the impression of being happy.

At the end of the dance she removed her bra. Her nipples were young and firm. She must have been eighteen or so. She came down among the audience and sat for a moment on the old men's laps, so they could fondle her breasts. When she was close to us she called out to Bino, 'You sex maniacs. Go home. You've been here all day.' She made a point of by-passing us, and disappeared into a cubicle on the other side of the stage.

Ching turned to me and said, 'Quick! quick! Join the queue. You'll get a free hand-job.'

I said to Wilson, 'Go on, give it a try.' But he would have been ashamed to do that with his compatriot.

If you went to the urinal you would pass the queue, half a dozen men, unembarrassed, indifferent, silent and unjoking. And through a gap in the plywood you could see the girl's hand at work, the standing man looking down at the girl's bowed head.

Meanwhile on stage the sex acts had begun. The Japanese girls were the least demonstrative, confining themselves to a routine striptease. The first Korean brought herself to a climax with a smooth white dildo. There was polite applause. The second Korean performed with mad aggression pretending to strangle herself with a length of cotton rope, and reaching a painful ecstasy with a large dildo covered with rubber points. She got a bit more response. She bowed politely and thanked the audience.

One of the Japanese girls reappeared. 'Those who would like to come on stage please raise your hands.' This would be the high point of the show, the cheapest available intercourse in Japan. There were six volunteers.

From their seats in the audience, the men began the elimination rounds by Jangkenpo: stone against paper, scissors versus stone, one round each to decide, no argument, no discussion, no sound at all. It was done very fast and it was astonishing to watch – the politeness, the efficiency, the breathtaking lack of emotion, and when the winner was found he betrayed not a single thought or feeling. Nobody congratulated him. Nobody seemed to envy him. It was as if nothing more was at stake than a bowl of noodles.

A large sheet and a pillow were spread out. The winner rose unhesitatingly from his seat, sat down on the platform to remove his shoes, which he placed neatly on stage as if entering a house. He loosened his tie. He was obviously a salaryman – and his lips went straight to the pale sagging breasts. As his tongue began to work, and the woman stroked his head, he seemed transformed into a child. He seemed to have surrendered everything to the woman, to be enveloped in her power, and she patted him and smiled and seemed to console him, as his tongue travelled down to her lap.

There he grew hungry. The woman spread her legs wider and an enka was played, adding a touch of melancholy to the scene. Minutes passed. I nudged Wilson. He shook his head slightly in disbelief. Bino and Ching craned forward. Their heads were only three feet away from the great meal that was being consumed. They inspected every detail, trying at the same time to preserve their composure. I found myself gulping.

The man stood up. He was thin, quite handsome, in his early thirties, dignified and with a studious manner. He took off his shirt and trousers indifferently and lay down on the sheet. The woman began to remove and fold his remaining clothes, which she placed at the side of the stage. It was very hygienic. She wiped him three times over with tissues, which she disposed of neatly in a plastic bag. She had changed from mother to nurse, as she expertly fitted the condom her head gracefully inclined to one side.

The act itself was speedily consumated. Once again, the man was scrupulously wiped clean and handed his clothes one by one. As he left the stage the woman bowed left and right to the audience, with one foot tucked behind the other, and thanked them for their attention. There was general applause. 'We're off,' I said to Bino.

'We're staying. We'll try for a ride in the next session.'

'Really?'

'Yeah, we've done it before. You shouldn't be ashamed of anything. We're all men.'

I thought, Well, they are lighter-skinned than me, and might just pass for Japanese. But supposing the next girl on stage was the Filipina, it would be shameful, for myself and for my country, to see her publicly fucked, particularly if the man doing it was a Filipino. Bino didn't think that. Filipino or Japanese, it made no difference to him, he said. But it made a difference to me, and it was obvious that the Filipina didn't like being seen at work by her compatriots. I tried to speak to her as we left. I wanted to say something friendly, something that would dispel the embarrassment between us. But she didn't want to talk. She had already formed her own opinion of the kind of people we were.

I thought about the other live show I'd seen in Tokyo, and how eager the audience was to get up on stage when the Filipinas appeared. I'd been naive before I came to Japan. I had thought that prostitution only existed in the Third World, that it was all a question of poverty. I hadn't realised that it also might be a question of affluence.

Outside, Wilson said, 'That was unbelievable. I never thought that such a thing existed in Japan. Japan really treats her women differently. It's really so different.'

I told him what Kazuo had said on the other occasion, as he secretly photographed the Filipinas on stage. 'This is tame,' he had said. 'A few years ago they used to perform with German Shepherds.'

13

A Stabbing

A SEPTEMBER STORM hit Yokohama, and all night the wind battered the rooftops. From my place on the tatami I watched the clouds swimming past and my laundry dancing on the line. The sliding window rattled irritatingly. I always kept it open, so that I would have something to see. The clouds continued, a parade of shapes, as if the whole universe were on the move. And from time to time I would think, If this weather continues, there'll be no work on the docks the next day.

Akihiro was short of funds again, and he had sneaked in last thing at night to doss in my room. He slept heavily, but the rattling window kept me awake.

At four I was startled by a shy tap at the door. I opened it gently so as not to disturb Akihiro. Jeff was outside, normally one of the calmest of my friends. He was calm now, and that very composure made me all the more agitated.

'What's the matter?' I asked.

He did not reply. I motioned him inside, closed the door and repeated the question. Jeff squatted on the tatami and lit a cigarette. He had been a soldier back home, before going AWOL, and he had retained a military manner. He was in no hurry to tell you what he knew – he never answered a question the first time around. I asked him softly a third time.

'There may be a raid,' he said.

I studied his face. 'What for?'

'There was a stabbing at the Manila Bar. A Japanese got knifed. Jun and Danny are in my room now. Paong and Daisy are packing their bags to be ready. They say it's better not to go out today.'

Rumours of raids in Koto were like rumours of coups back home – there were lots of them, but some were true. And there was always a reason: excessive noise, a street-fight, a stabbing incident. One man's action might jeopardise the whole community.

The previous month, for instance, one of Rogelio's mates had held a birthday party in the building where I had spent my first night in Koto. The Japanese neighbours had complained and the immigration agents had arrived early the next morning. They'd brought a coach big enough for fifty prisoners and they cordoned off the building. Rogelio himself was nabbed when he answered a knock at the door, thinking it was one of his mates. Others had been found cooking or brushing their teeth. The agents had scored six out of ten Filipinos. One man had escaped simply by remaining on the lavatory. One was wise enough not to open his door. The other two fought with the agents and escaped. They had laughed about this afterwards, saying the agents were too young, no match for them. We had passed round the hat on behalf of those who were deported.

The fact that Jun had taken refuge in Jeff's room was surprising, since they were not close friends. Jun was one of the Banana Boys, and a close friend of the Banana sacho, 'Khomeini', but he seldom put work in our direction, although he controlled several jobs. In his free time he would hang out with the Bataan gang, who would come to his room for a game of poker, a cough syrup session or to watch porno videos. He had invited me there only once, and I was amused to see that one wall was plastered with religious images – the Virgin Mary and the *balbasang Kristo*, the Bearded Christ – while opposite there hung full-length posters of Japanese starlets in bikinis. The porn-film was in progress. I said to Jun, 'Don't you think Jesus Christ will be seduced by these girls?' but he rebuked me sternly. 'Tisoy,' he said, 'never say that again. Jesus Christ is my brother.'

It was religion that brought him and Danny together. They would read the Bible and exchange verses. Jun had nearly become a priest – he was a respected local preacher back home in Cavite, before his marriage – and he had not lost his religious fervour. It existed naturally alongside the other elements of his life – the small-time gangsterism, the drug-taking, the pornography. The key to his influence with Khomeini, the Banana Sacho, was that he introduced him to girls, acting as interpreter using the little Nihonggo that he possessed. This visibly transformed Khomeini's life, causing him to brush his teeth for the first time, to dress smartly and wear perfume. A new light came into his face – before he had been a typical lonely unmarriageable type. Now, with Jun's skill at procuring, he suddenly seemed to decide that things weren't so bad. He began to favour Filipinos at the gemba, and we knew what was going on in the bars when he complained to us one day that whenever he met a Filipina it always seemed to be her birthday.

We found Jun and Danny in Jeff's room. She was cowering like a shivering chicken. Jun looked as if he'd had the wind knocked out of him, and at first he was unwilling to say what had happened. But eventually he relented.

On Saturday night, after a day unloading bananas on the Tokyo pier, a group of them had gone to the Manila Bar. They had been drinking for some time and were watching the video screen of the karaoke, singing along with the projected words. Jun was a close friend of Romero, the Fashion Model, and Paong, the Joker. They were at one table. Near them sat a man called Benito, whom I knew slightly, having worked with him on the bananas myself.

He was from the Bataan gang and was one of the pioneers of Koto, having jumped ship several years before. He didn't strike me as a particularly violent man.

In the early hours of the morning a Japanese man arrived with two Filipinas in tow. If you saw someone like that, you would always presume he might be a papa-san or a Yakuza. The Japanese was already drunk and vociferous. He kept cursing, but exactly what he was saying was not clear. In the Philippines we may curse a lot in our own company, but if you are in public, in a restaurant or bar, and you hear somebody cursing a lot at the next table, you take it as a sign of disrespect to everyone else in the room. Resentment builds up. You feel the man is arrogant and ought to be taught a lesson.

The Manila Bar felt like Filipino territory. Although it was owned by a Japanese, it was staffed by Pinoys of dubious legality and served San Miguel beer and our native dishes.

Whatever the Japanese man was saying, Benito would be likely to understand more of it than the rest, since he spoke very good Nihonggo. After a while he began to say, 'I'm going to hit that man.' His brother and sister told him to ignore the provocation. The man was just drunk. But then Benito stood up and when his brother tried to restrain him, said, 'Even though you're my brother, if you try to stop me I'll hit you instead.'

He had his *beinte-nueve*, his butterfly knife, ready as he went over to the table and seemed at first to embrace the Japanese, who was larger than him and struggled to his feet. At this point, Jun said, Benito 'horsed' the man – that is, he rode on him, with one arm clinging to his neck and with his free hand stabbed him six times in the back.

The girls screamed. The Japanese fell to the floor, blood spurting, and everyone fled. As they tried to find taxis, the police were already swarming all over the area.

The owner of the bar knew most of the clients, and where they lived. The next night, Jun and Danny returned from a disco to find that Paong and Daisy had been investigated, photographed and fingerprinted in their room. Immediately, they had packed and moved out. The police had known the number of their room, they knew that Paong was a witness and that the couple were illegal, but oddly they had not taken them into custody. All Jun knew about the Japanese was that he was now in hospital.

I told just a little of this to Akihiro as we set out to work. I was reluctant to be on the streets, but I felt I ought to find out what was going on.

Khomeini, the Banana sacho, shook his finger at me. 'No Filipinos today,' he said, 'too dangerous.'

'Why, sacho?'

'The man stabbed at the Manila,' he said, drawing

a finger across his throat, 'already dead. The police are after the Filipinos.'

Akihiro grew agitated and tried to ask for more details, but Khomeini didn't want to talk. We went back to my room fast.

An ugly row developed between us. Akihiro was keen to know everything that had happened, but I didn't want to tell him. I felt forced into a position of defending my people and their interests. Whenever these incidents occurred, I would feel ashamed for my people. From the smallest provocations to the largest – cheating the laundry machine, using Filipino money on the train, shoplifting, changing fake dollars, robbery, street-brawling and stabbing – we were always giving grounds for our deportation.

Akihiro had taken the stabbing as being an insult by the Filipinos against the Japanese people. He wanted to know the culprit. I knew, but I didn't know in fact who was to blame, and a part of me could sympathise with Benito. I knew what it was like to want to hit an arrogant insulting Japanese. So I kept quiet.

It was as if Akihiro had put the argument on a war footing. There was more than a hint of the Greater Japanese Co-Prosperity Sphere. Akihiro said, 'The Filipinos do not know the Japanese. You don't know us! You don't know our culture. You don't know our language. You don't know Japanese society. But when we stand up and unite, you will not only be enemies to us. You'll be babies!' And he dismissed my people with a gesture of scorn.

Akihiro phoned the police to discover that the victim was still alive, but in a coma. He pursued his investigations. He went to the Manila Bar, but it was shut down for a week. Finally the community opened up a little, and he was able to discover what I already knew.

During the first week after the stabbing, none of the banana sachos would hire Filipinos, but in the end they were forced to relent. They had boatloads of bananas and nobody to unload them. But life had not yet returned to normal. The victim was still in a critical condition and Benito had not yet been caught.

On the first day that we went back to the banana ships, some men arrived during the afternoon break and took Jun off for questioning in the workers' canteen. Immediately the sachos came and told us to hide in the hold. The interrogation took an hour. The men, whoever they were, knew exactly where Jun lived and that he had been at the bar that night, but Jun claimed not to have seen exactly what had happened.

As soon as the coast was clear, we knocked off work, and in the ensuing days there began a cat and mouse game involving Filipinos and their sachos and the investigators. One day, after the men had arrived and looked down at the workers in the hold, the sachos said, 'They may be waiting outside with a van.' So the company laid on a tug, and the workers escaped to another pier. The more the work was interrupted, the more desperate the banana sachos became. One, pointing at me, said, 'You! don't take your helmet off!' He was hoping to make me less conspicuous, seen from above, with my dark skin. My mates would tease me not to go near the palette as it was lifted by the crane but to stay down near the edge of the hold, out of view. Above our heads the sachos stood on guard, and if we looked up inquiringly, they would say, 'Don't worry. Keep on working. They're not here.'

We would eat together huddled in the company van, and on the way to and from the worksite we would slouch out of view, with our helmets over our eyes, and because the sachos believed that we were being monitored at the tollgates they would tell us not to make a noise or speak any Filipino as we passed through.

Paong was still in hiding. Now Romero, another witness, went off to find work in Tokyo. Only Jun remained in his room, resigned to the possibility of arrest.

Then, to our amazement, Benito himself was seen on the streets of Kotobuki. I saw him standing on the corner, talking to other members of the Bataan gang, his arms folded across his chest, as if nothing had happened. I passed by without a word. None of the rest of us wanted to have anything to do with him.

'He's got a nerve,' said Manny, 'coming here like that.' Generally, we wanted Benito arrested, to take the pressure off us. Indeed, we would have liked to see the last of all the gangsters and petty criminals. The last few weeks had demonstrated that we were literally irreplaceable as workers, but any criminal incident turned the whole community into outlaws. A strange kind of outlaw: the bananas I had been unloading had been grown by Filipinos in Mindanao, transported on ships with Filipino crews, and handled by Filipinos in the docks of Yokohama. The only thing we didn't do with these outsize, uniform, intensely cultivated, tasteless fruit was eat them. We despised them. We used to mock the Japanese for eating them – the favourite fruit of monkeys!

Nobody would have gone so far as to shop Benito to the police. He went off to Tokyo, where we learnt he was working on the same gemba as Romero. Not only that. One night, the television news carried a report of the investigation, showing footage of a building in which the hunted man was supposed to be living. Silhouetted in the lighted window was the familiar figure of Romero, the Fashion Model.

It seemed to me extraordinary that the investigation was taking so long. The police knew their territory well – they had communications boxes on every block. Even the trees of the city were numbered. Everything was accounted for. And yet the case dragged on, until one day Benito, Romero and a friend were captured at the most obvious place, the gemba.

We were all relieved. The two friends were immediately deported, and Benito's case was taken up by the Communists and the other support groups. He spent more than a year in jail, while his victim recovered and an out of court settlement was reached.

During this time, the owner of the Manila Bar was arrested for dealing in crack, and Tito, a neighbour of Benito, was eventually jailed for his part in the affair. The Manila Bar was closed down for good – the only place in Yokohama that had sported the flag of the Philippines.

When I got back to Manila, finding that I had connections with both Tito and Benito's families, I went to see them in Bataan. Tito's family was living in penury, the children thin, the mother almost speechless with misery. With some difficulty, she asked me if it was true that Tito was living with somebody. I couldn't tell her what I knew: that he had stopped working and become the henpecked lover of a prostitute. He spent the day cooking, doing the laundry, cleaning their small room, and drinking cough syrup with the Bataan gang.

The gloomy house, concrete throughout, with its fancy balustrade and its panelled rooms hung with grimy Saudi rugs, was proof that they had once been reasonably well off. Tito's wife and mother-in-law began to cry in unison. It was like a funeral dirge, laced with Spanish curses from the mother-in-law: *bastardo, puneta, puta*. She had been well off before; she had sold a number of fishing boats to finance Tito's trip to Japan; other men sent remittances home; Tito had sent nothing in all his two years away; the fishing industry had collapsed; there were no other men in the family; she was reduced to borrowing money here and there.

Tito's encounter with Japan had brought ruin on his family. At Benito's home, we couldn't talk openly, because the children didn't know that their father was in prison. They didn't seem badly off: neither Tito nor Benito had gone to Japan because they couldn't find work or support themselves back home. Indeed, it was generally true that it was the lower middle classes rather than the very poor who were drawn into the world of Kotobuki. It was only they who could raise the money for the initial payments – the papers and the air-tickets and the bribes. You could not really say that necessity had driven these people into the Japanese underground. They had gone there not to make money but to make *more* money, not for their daily bread but for the finer things in life.

Romero, for instance, with all his jewellery – the Fashion Model, the playboy, who had been deported at the time of Benito's arrest. Many months later I met him in the passport office in Manila. He looked dreadful. Gone were the rings and the bracelets, gone all the gold. His face was unshaven and his clothes were a mess. He had a clutch of passports which he showed me. He had become a pimp, recruiting girls for the entertainment world. And he had a fake name and a new passport. As soon as he could he would be back in Japan.

14

Love, Death, Etcetera

ON MY WAY home, on the underground platform, a serious-looking woman approached me and asked in Japanese if I had time to spare. I asked her why. 'I want to pray for you,' she said in English.

'Why do you want to pray for me?'

'I want you ... attain salvation. I want you go heaven.'

'Can't you pray for me here?' I said, indicating the platform.

'It's better in the church. More blessings in the church.'

'God is not in the church,' I said philosophically.

'I want you alleluiah. I want you salvation. Only ten minutes, I pray for you.'

'Well, I'm sorry,' I said finally, 'I don't have ten minutes today.'

Neng is the pretty, nineteen-year-old daughter of my

friend Ronny. She opened the door while reading a letter from home. 'Oh,' she exclaimed, 'she's given birth already. A girl again. What?' And ignoring her visitors she began to count, 'February, March, April ... Now October – it was only just after the last one. It's my sister. "Please send me a lapad," she says. She hasn't written anything except "Please send me a lapad".'

She works in a computer-chip factory, assembling circuits. She's only paid half a lapad a day, very low by Japanese standards. But she says it's better to be paid less than to have to put up with curses and obscenities.

'I don't want to work in a bar,' she said. 'I can't bear it. They're full of leeches. I once tried, and the customers kept saying I had a flat breast. I prefer the factory. My sacho and co-workers are kind. But I always bring a knife with me. *This* ... ' she produced a butterfly knife from her bag ' ... is to protect myself. The Japanese are scared of knives. Once you show them one, they run away. They always think they are *ichiban* (number one). But they are only ichiban in money.'

Ronny, her father, works – he says – as an 'arsonist'. Every day he burns a mountain of rubbish and crushes hundreds of 'old' cars. The flat he shares with Neng is furnished entirely with *gomi* – all the appliances, the telephone, the china, the cutlery, blankets, furniture – everything came off the tip, where he works twelve hours a day, seven days a week. The long hours are obligatory (none of us can ever ask to change a work schedule) but the Sunday overtime is something else. Ronny works like a Japanese, and his face and arms are scratched as if he'd been fighting a hundred cats. He's working he says, not for himself but for his 'women', and the kids he has had by them.

Neng is his daughter by his first 'woman', his wife. But Neng says Ronny never remits anything to her mother. Neng herself has become the family breadwinner since her arrival in Japan a year before her father. What Ronny means by working for his women is his two mistresses in Manila, and their kids. He left a regular job in Manila in order to come to Japan, and within a year Neng and Ronny had six-teen relatives living in the neighbourhood, Saitama Prefecture, which is adjacent to Tokyo. More were on the way. Neng's sister wanted to join them, but her children were still young. The clan had all found regular factory jobs, to which they were ferried every day by the recruiters' van.

The speed with which this family had establish-ed itself in the labour underground was exceptional in my experience. Most of them were educated, some even ex-government employees, and all of them seemed secure enough and happy to be doing manual work. The police had made checks on Ronny and

Neng's apartment, and they seemed content not to hassle them. Indeed, Saitama Prefecture was well-known for employing illegal labour, and there are many Filipina entertainers in the bars.

One day Ronny was at work sorting out aluminium from the heaps of scrap-metal when a Japanese worker pointed a powerful hose in his direction. It was a painful joke and, Ronny said, 'if we'd been in the Philippines I'd have decapitated him. But when the Japanese make fun of you you can't take revenge. You can't fight with them. If you do, you'll get arrested. You'll pay a huge sum. But let them come to our place, they'd be dead in a second.'

Neng comes home from work singing, '*Huwag kang iibig sa sakang. Huwag kang iibig sa supot.*' Don't fall in love with a bow-legged man. Don't fall in love with an uncircumcised man. She doesn't take the Japanese seriously. She mocks both men and women.

She thinks the girls are too subservient to the men. She picks up the ashtray, puts it in front of her mouth like a fan and giggles, the way the girls do. She imitates them on the telephone, polite and meekly bowing. She is constantly watching and imitating. Japan is not her sort of place. She misses her mother. When she has enough money she will go home and put herself through college. She has no intention of marrying here, and when she sees me off at the bus-stop she is still singing, '*Huwag kang iibig sa sakang. Huwag kang iibig sa supot.'*

They're always saying that Japan is a very peaceful country. You can walk the streets at night with nothing to fear. No hold-ups, robbers, rapists, urban guerrillas, cheating taxi-drivers . . .

Japan is a beautiful country; but countries not like Japan are also beautiful.

'Would you like our country to be like Japan?' a friend asked me.

'Not really,' I said. 'I just want my country to be a better Philippines.'

'What do you think of Manila?' I asked Kiyoe, a student, just returned from the Philippines.

'I don't like it,' she said. 'It's *kitanai, kusai, urusai*.' Dirty, smelly, noisy.

What she said was true. I was expecting her in return to ask me how I liked Koto. I would have said the same. I would have told her the truth.

I'm standing on the deck of a cargo ship, knackered, after unloading hundreds of boxes of bananas from the Philippines. I pee into the rusty waters of Tokyo Bay. Hundreds of jellyfish, like miniature, pulsating parachutes, rise and fall in the wash of the great ships. They can survive in all this shit.

There is a park on the dockside, and I can see the sun setting behind the naked cherry trees. All day at work in the hold of the ship, without being able to see, as we say, even the cheek of the sky. Then suddenly all this space, all this colour, all this beauty.

The police came to Koto this morning, to the place where we gather as Standing Men every day. They came in two patrol cars and an ambulance. They saw us and we saw them. We didn't run or hide and they ignored us. No arrest was made.

They had come to pick up the body of a day-labourer who had died under the steps of the Labour Centre. It's a place where several down-and-outs spend the day drinking, and their faces become blackened with the smoke of the improvised fires. This is the second time I have seen someone carried away from there on a cold morning. As soon as we heard the siren of the ambulance, we knew it was either a death or an accident, and we didn't have to hide. It wasn't meant for us.

The judo holds us in silence on the black-and-white TV: Japan versus South Korea. It's the Seoul Olympics and the Koreans are winning more gold medals than the Japanese. We are in the dining cabin of a South Korean cargo ship, having just finished our lunch of fish, pickles and rice.

There are only about four Japanese present, including the sacho: we are in Korean territory, with a dozen Korean crew and three Koto Koreans working with us, unloading steel bars. The four of us Filipinos want the Koreans to win. We identify with the under-dog. But we are also not at liberty to cheer in front of our employer. We mutter encouragement to the Korean side. Everybody else – Korean or Japanese – is silent.

The Koreans lose.

Jinky, the prostitute who had left one sadistic Japan-ese boyfriend in order to take up with a Filipino sadist, bled for several weeks during her pregnancy and was in and out of hospital. She hated lying in bed all day and having blood samples taken by a nurse who insisted on talking English, which Jinky didn't understand. Besides, she said, if she delivered in hospital, she would be charged ¥250,000 (over a thousand pounds). 'If I'd delivered there last night,' she told me, after discharging herself, 'I'd have left the baby with them as payment.'

She'd been seven years in Japan without getting caught, but her family believed her to be single and going straight. She couldn't have gone back to Manila to have the child, without her father finding out, but the trouble with staying at home was that Randy still wanted to have sex with her, and would cut up rough if refused. She spent a lot of time keeping out of his way, and was always relieved when he found a day's work, which wasn't often, because he was used to being kept by her, and because he refused to do any job other than *banana*, and then only with his mates.

So Jinky stayed at home, bleeding and trying not to get beaten up, and one day she went to the toilet and to her surprise gave birth to the first Filipino to be born in Kotobuki. The landlord called an ambulance, and one of the first things the hospital did was register the child's birth. So the baby had a blue card although the parents did not. It was a legitimate illegitimate baby, and the fact that it had legal status gave its parents some measure of protection.

Koto was extremely short of babies, and this newcomer caused a small sensation on the streets, particularly in the eyes of the old men, the *oji-chans*, who used to give the little boy money. The parents too were doting; in the case of Randy, who had a wife and two daughters at home, the affection was compounded by the fact that the boy resembled him to a startling degree. Randy, unusually for a Filipino, had a thick beard and a moustache. The child, born with a full head of hair, had a five-o'clock shadow in a fine silky blonde. The father took great delight in wheeling his first son around Kotobuki, and prophesying great things for him. 'When he's seven,' he said, 'I'll make him a man. I'll teach him how to fuck.' It was Randy's intention that, when he and Jinky eventually returned to the Philippines, *he* would keep the child. He and Jinky knew that they would not stay together indefinitely – indeed, Jinky often wanted to get away from Randy. He was a shit, but he was handsome, more handsome than she – as a plain girl and a prostitute – felt she had a right to expect. She too was determined to keep the child. And so the future battle was prepared for in a very loving way, with both parents showering affection on their baby. Randy, the toughie, the *brusko*, was the last person you would have expected as a doting father, changing nappies and making baby-talk. But he had achieved his great ambition, and he wasn't going to let go. He would say proudly, 'Finally, I got a son. Of all places, in Japan!'

'What do you like most in Japan,' I was asked.

'I like your trees,' I said, 'and I like the way you take care of them. I like your stamps and your handmade postcards. My friends are so pleased to receive them. I like your tatamis and paper sliding doors. I like your fairness, your hospitality and your sense of nationalism.'

At the docks, a Japanese stevedore asked me, 'Do you think there are also bad people in Japan?'

'Of course,' I said. 'No country on earth has a monopoly on Goodness.'

'But in Japan,' the man insisted, 'there are very few *dorobo* (thieves) or *usotsuki* (liars).'

I'm standing in front of the *ofuro* after my evening bath, waiting for friends who are still inside. Across the road, in front of the Korean *snakku*, two drunken old labourers are pushing and pulling at each other like sumo wrestlers. One of them gets pushed off the edge of the pavement. He struggles to his feet. Then they're back wrestling again.

Meanwhile two shaven-headed Yakuzas come out of the video gambling parlour, walking as if they own Kotobuki, as if the street is made for them. The younger one walks a couple of paces behind. Maybe they are *oyabun* and *kobun*, master and pupil. They are familiar faces around here and they are also drunk.

They see the two old men fighting and, without a word, at lightning speed, the older gangster jumps in, grabs one of them by the hair and hits him in the face with all his might. The force of the blow throws him several feet, to near the entrance of the snack bar. Fallen, he coils his body like a foetus and covers his face with his hands.

Now the oyabun begins kicking the old man in the face and stomach, wherever he can. The other man who had been fighting makes himself scarce, the clients leave the snakku and the crowd forms to watch from a respectful distance. The younger gangster, the kobun, doesn't join in. It is as if he were being given a demonstration, as the old man groans and weeps, with blood pouring from his face, until finally he lies unconscious by the wall.

Done with his victim, but not yet satisfied, the oyabun goes inside the empty bar, overturns every table and smashes all the chairs, breaking every glass and destroying anything within reach. Nobody stops him. Nobody calls the police or the ambulance. We are all spectators. We are the dregs of Japanese society.

One of the restaurants beneath Yokohama station offers German beer in boot-shaped glasses. Bobby, one of the young veterans of Koto, his Japanese girlfriend Midori, Mayumi and I are trying it out: if you're not careful, the air entering the toe of the boot causes the beer to spill out over your shirt. It's the first time we've all been out together, and I've only just been introduced to Mayumi. She seems very friendly and cheerful. Occasionally, I notice, her elbow comes to rest on my shoulder. Bobby and Midori aren't talking much. Maybe they've had a row. I'm photographing them across the table, but it takes several shots before they can be persuaded to smile.

On our side of the table it's as if we've known each other quite a long time, and before we split up I ask Mayumi for her address. She writes it in my notebook, along with her telephone number, which was what I was after.

I know that Mayumi travels every day from Yoko-hama to university in Tokyo. I try the phone number. Fortunately, Mayumi gets to the phone before her mother. I explain (this is a kind of lie) that I have to go to Akihiro's office the next day. Maybe we could meet up at Ishikawa station and travel up together?

On the train, Mayumi asks me how long I will be staying in Japan.

'Maybe until December,' I say. 'I want to see the snow. I want to see Filipinos working in the snow. But ... ' I paused, 'if I had some reason to stay longer ... then ... '

Mayumi suddenly says, 'If I asked you to stay longer, what would you do?'

'*Will* you ask me to do that?' I say. I feel as if my heart has suddenly announced: Ladies and gentlemen, this is the moment you have all been waiting for.

'I'll have to think about it,' she replies, and turns to look out of the window at Kawasaki City. My stop is just coming up.

'How long can you wait?' Mayumi asks me.

'Three years,' I say. We often have this con-versation.

'But I'm not sure if you *can* wait,' says Mayumi. She is melancholy today. 'You're a playboy. Even though I'm with you, you can't resist looking at beautiful girls. Sometimes it insults me.'

'But I just look at them,' I argue, 'no more, no less. Because they are pretty, I have to look at them. It's natural to appreciate beauty. Even you, you like to be appreciated.'

15

Zaldy's Advice

AT KANNAI STATION, a great gate spans the width
of Isezaki-cho, and from the gate hangs a replica of
a sailing ship. This is where the foreign seamen in
Yokohama come window-shopping – Russians, main-
land Chinese, Latinos, Filipinos. They look so poor in
comparison with our lot from Kotobuki, staring at the
electronic goods and shaking their heads at the prices.
To us, to be white is to be rich. The Russians form
the exception to this rule, and their poverty provides
a topic of conversation at the jobsite. It seems strange
to us that they can come from a superpower and yet be
so poor. They work on their rusty ships without gloves
or safety shoes. Sometimes we feel pity for them, and
leave our gloves behind for them to use.

Isezaki-cho, a broad, tree-lined street, leads up
from one McDonalds to the next. In the alleys
off to the right lie the *o-mises* and prostitution
dens where the Filipinas work, and where most

of the illegal immigrants lose their money: Dandy, Sopurando ('Soapland'), Sauna, Manila Bar – their names announced with large neon signs. Some of the establishments carry notices in English and Tagalog banning Filipinos. We are said to be troublemakers.

The Japanese pimps in this area look like waiters, with white shirts and black bow ties. They are touting for custom at the various love hotels. The girls are not allowed to walk the streets, but outside the o-mises there are usually a few to call you in. It is strange to be addressed in Japanese by a Filipina, but the rule is that conversation on the street must be conducted in Japanese. Once you're inside the bar, and have bought the girl a drink, you are allowed to revert to your native language.

The further of the two McDonalds has become a Filipino rendez-vous. A dozen guys from Kotobuki are hanging around outside, together with members of a rock band – long-haired and in studded leather. A couple of girls in shorts sit smoking ostentatiously and eyeing the passers-by. Their manner is calculated and malicious; they are veterans of the trade. Nearby – a rare sight – sits a couple with a baby. They are illegal too, but they cannot be deported until their baby is one year old.

For the rest, I look at the group and think: these people could be arrested at any moment; there's no escape route. Manny has the same thought: 'They're very daring. And those girls, the way they display themselves outside – it's shameful. That's why the Japanese look down on us.'

Manny, Wilson and I have come out disguised as tourists. Wilson has a Canon F-1 which we bought in Shinjuku last week for the staggering price of ¥150,000. Manny has a Nikon FG with a 200mm zoom lens. Mine is an old Olympus OM-2, picked up in Tokyo. We're all wearing Adidas 'French' training shoes, which Manny acquired at half price from a Pinoy who worked at the factory. The rest of our kit comes from the flea market, but we take care to look well turned out.

The use of a camera as a prop was my idea, which began as a security measure and turned into a craze. In Koto, the possession of a real camera is quite a status symbol, but to know how to use it is something else again.

We go to the Tropicana Restaurant, an upstairs establishment opposite McDonalds. One of several places in the area selling Filipino food, it has the advantage of not being visible from the street. You would never find it unless someone took you there. It seats a dozen people at most. The owner, a very friendly Japanese, has travelled around the tropics and can cook Indonesian, Thai and Filipino food. You can specify the ingredients you want, and some-times he will throw in some extra rice free.

At our table, we ostentatiously display our cam-eras. The owner knows our regular drinks – San

Miguel beer for Wilson and me, gin and tonic for Manny, who can't drink beer without going red in the face. We are still on our first round when Zaldy bursts into the restaurant and comes up to our table. 'I'll just stay here for a while,' he says. 'I'm hiding from someone.'

He is bleary-eyed and apprehensive, glancing around him while under the table he shakes a small bottle. I know at once that it's cough syrup. He knocks it back in two quick gulps. 'This is 120cc,' he says. 'That's nothing. It'll take effect in twenty minutes.'

I slip into his language. 'How often do you hit?' I ask.

'I get a charge every day.' He pockets the bottle.

The syrup, which is available only on prescription in the Philippines, can be bought freely in Japan. The bottles resemble the common tonic Lipovitan, so addicts remove the labels and drink in public places, although this can be dangerous.

'Do you want a drink?'

'No,' says Zaldy, 'it only lowers the kick.'

As the syrup begins to take effect, he becomes talkative in a dreamy sort of way. He's an ugly man, with bad teeth and a habit of rolling his dentures in his mouth. He likes baggy clothes which balloon around his boney frame. He always carries a butterfly knife. He wears dark glasses to church, and quite a lot of gold. He walks with a stoop, and with his hands thrust deep into his pockets.

Physically he is a mess, but nobody would pick a fight with him. You'd win the first round, but you'd soon find you'd made a lot of enemies. Zaldy's connections extend beyond the circle of his Laguna province-mates. They include drug addicts from every major region, and this network of connections seems to give him a special confidence. If a fight breaks out, he won't move out of the way – he'll stand there and watch, secure in the knowledge that he won't be touched.

He's been in Koto almost two years, and considers himself a veteran. First of all, he specialised in looking after the new recruits his brother sent over from Manila, and he fleeced them for his services. But as more and more Filipinos arrived in Koto, and the community wised up, it became impossible for people like Zaldy to charge a 'shokai fee' (for the introduction to the job). He adapted to this situation well, and was in fact quite generous in telling you where the work was. He believed that if work was available it should be shared by everyone, and he hated the Iglesia ni Kristo mob for the greed with which they cornered jobs. He often threatened that one day there would be a reckoning.

He lives one door away from a police station, and has been arrested more than once, but somehow he always manages to get released. On one occasion he escaped an immigration agent by hitting him as hard as possible on the hand. He doesn't fear arrest any more. 'The police know me by now,' he says. He hardly works. Maybe I've seen him three times at the jobsite.

'How old do you think I am?' he asks.

'Twenty-two,' says Manny.

'Twenty-five,' I say.

'You're both wrong,' he replies, as if this were something of a revelation. 'I'm twenty-three.' He reckons he can impress us with his curriculum vitae. 'Before coming to Japan I worked in Hongkong and Brunei. Japan's the best. In Hongkong I always feel scared. In Brunei you will starve. Here you are free . . . '

He glances again at the door. Now he seems in a hurry.

'My sugar mommy is waiting outside. She's talking with friends. Miguel and August are looking after her. I came here because when we're together she won't let me get a charge. She's fifty-six, two years older than my mother.'

He says this quite casually and I recoil at the thought. But Zaldy seems to expect us to be impressed. He's patronising us, telling us what we're missing out on.

'I haven't worked for three months,' he continues. 'She supports me. She gives me expensive clothes, chains, rings and things. The first time I fucked her she gave me ¥30,000. But the second time she didn't give me anything. A friend passed her on.

'I don't use what she gives me. I sell all the jewellery, and I send all the clothes back home for my brother to sell. I used to do the same job in the Philippines, but only with gays.'

So Zaldy had been what the Japanese call a *hosto*. I'd met another former hosto on the jobsite. He'd worked in Shinjuku, where there are several gay bars, advertised by billboards bearing full-length portraits of the supposedly available men in a variety of macho poses, with a variety of invented names and ages.

High on syrup, Zaldy looks an unlikely hosto, from the point of view of either sex. He manipulates his dentures with his tongue, as if he's going to eat them.

'If you just get dressed up a bit,' he tells us, 'I can introduce you to a sugar mommy. Never waste your money in the o-mise. They'll only fool you there. Look at Bert. He's been deceived. If you want girls, not from the o-mise. There's no hope there. My advice is – target any Filipinas married to Japanese. Never mind if they're not beautiful. As long as you think you can get something from them, do it!'

This is the special area of the sexual market that Zaldy and his friends have identified and targeted, and as in other matters Zaldy is generous. He is the *sungkit* king of Koto. A sungkit is a hook, and we use the term to denote any kind of tampering with the coin laundry, the tumble dryer and the stove. He is proud of his skill with a piece of bent wire, and he has passed his skills on to the rest of us. Now he is sharing his skills as the other kind of hooker.

He gets up, full of confidence and cough syrup. 'Tonight,' he says, 'I am going to take my sugar mommy to my room.'

The food has not yet arrived. I slip outside to see what the sugar mommy looks like. Miguel and August are still chatting her up, while Zaldy keeps a slight distance, as if not wishing to betray their relationship. She's dressed in black jeans and a floral blouse, with large dark glasses which she adjusts from time to time. I was expecting to see a much rougher type – a *mama-san*, a *matrona* – but somehow I get the impression that this is a woman of education and background. She has a teenage girl with her, who seems to add respectability to the scene, like a brilliant prop. There is no hint of any sexual assignation.

I stand by the telephone booth, pretending to be about to make a call. McDonalds is on the left. We are proud, as Filipinos, that we had a McDonalds before the Japanese did – or so we think. A great deal of status is attached to the place. It takes money and it takes courage to visit McDonalds in Manila – courage, because the waiters address you in English.

We save the wrappers and the plastic cups, anything with the logo. We put the cups on display in the *sala*. We decorate our schoolbooks with the wrappers. And in Japan, we risk arrest in order to be seen at McDonalds. We will do anything for that little bit of status.

16

Sumimasen, Gommennasai

THE SKY WAS full of interesting things – airplanes, helicopters, crows, swallows and falling leaves. Normally, for security reasons, we would have taken our break inside the gemba, but the interest of what was going on in the sky seemed to lure us out into the open. Every day there were two queer objects floating overhead – low-flying, slow-moving and looking like oversized fish-balloons. One was advertising Asahi beer, the other Konica film.

Pungay was wondering how they worked. Maybe, he said, there's a small airplane inside the balloon. But they were so slow I said maybe it was a kind of helicopter. My mind was far away. I was feeling lonely and homesick. Perhaps we both were. Gazing at the sky as we drank our coffee, looking at the autumn trees, the helicopters and these strange things had brought this mood upon us. 'Maybe,' I said philosophically, 'it's the wind that keeps them afloat.'

'What's the difference between a train ride and a plane ride?' asked Pungay. And then he answered the question himself. 'On a plane ride, all you can see are the clouds. With a train ride you get scenery and pretty girls. But a train ride is ordinary. A plane ride is something to be proud of.' He gestured rather grandly with his can of coffee as he developed this thought, and at the end of every sentence he paused and smiled and seemed to encourage approval. Pungay had only once been on a plane, two years before, coming to Japan. He was in his late twenties, but he liked to talk like an old man. He liked wisdom. His way of expressing disapproval would be to say, 'You can't learn anything from listening to him.'

The thought progressed in an easy, dreamy way. 'Riding in an airplane is often not as beautiful as we think it's going to be. But . . . ' here he rose to the theme, '*it is a beautiful part of one's personal history*. In our country . . . ' (he was always telling me things like this which I knew already; he liked explaining how his stereo worked, and demonstrating the karaoke) ' . . . in our country, very few people have experienced or can afford an airplane ride. So our children . . . ' (he had been married a year before coming here and was so far childless) '. . . will boast to their friends that their parents have been abroad and have flown in airplanes. They will be proud of their parents.' And then an unpleasant thought struck him. 'But then their friends will ask – isn't it that those who go abroad do so because they don't have money?'

'No,' I said, 'I'll tell my children that we went abroad not because we didn't have money, but because we wanted to earn *more* money.'

This seemed to satisfy him. Pungay (the nickname means Tantalising Eyes — he earned it one night when he was drunk) was from a family of landed farmers. His brothers and sisters were in the professions, and he had a degree in agriculture. His parents-in-law were in America, and his wife wanted to go there as well. He was somewhat worried about this. It was hard to see, if she went, how they were going to get together again, and therefore a little hard to see where these children were going to come from.

But there we sat, dreaming of our unborn children, who would be proud of us someday for what we were doing now. My nose had been streaming all day, and the cold stung my lips like lemon in a wound. We were so wrapped up in these thoughts that we didn't notice the policeman until his motorbike was a few yards away.

He came straight to the point, without the usual polite apology or preliminaries. 'Are you Japanese?'

I bowed and answered No in my meekest voice.

He approached me cautiously, as if ready to grab my arm if I started to run for it. 'Country where?' he said.

'I'm Filipino.'

'Passport!' He thrust out his hand. I could see Pungay slowly walking back to the worksite, with studied relaxation, putting on his helmet as he went, for better disguise. Oh come on, Pungay, I thought, don't leave me.

'I didn't bring it,' I said. 'It's in my room.'

'Visa what?'

'Student visa.'

'School what?' This was the question I dreaded. I didn't want to get my school into trouble.

By now Pungay, with his helmet well thrust down over his features, was disappearing behind the site toilet. The policeman put his hand on my arm and slowly tightened his grip. I didn't speak. I pretended not to understand any further questions. '*Gommennasai*,' I'm sorry, I said, and '*Sumimasen*,' I beg your pardon. And I kept bowing and bowing. As the policeman sensed that I wasn't going to run for it, he relaxed his grip slightly.

I'd lived in fear of this moment for the last nine months, but now that it came I was surprised how calm I felt. I was strangely confident that as long as I showed no resistance at all he would let me off. A saying from Zen passed through my mind: 'The strong wind blows, the bamboo bends.' If I was deported – well, that was that. It was inherent in our status. I had only one regret – I would be separated from Mayumi after only a few weekends together.

What would happen to our relationship after I left Japan? How would she react?

'Is he also a Filipino?' said the policeman, pointing to where Pungay had been.

I hesitated. 'Yes,' I said. He told me to look for him, and released my arm. Pungay was smoking nervously behind the latrine. 'You shouldn't have come here,' he said. 'Look,' I said, 'he's only going to ask us a few questions.' 'Are you sure?' 'Yes, come on.' I could see two other Filipinos hiding further away. Pungay had already warned them.

We walked with him up the hill. Because he had to push his old-fashioned motorbike, we were free to try to make a dash for it, but instead we stayed with him, silent and submissive. Pungay and I were determined not to do anything to arouse his suspicions.

The police post was a small office with one table and three chairs, and a cloakroom where he hung his coat and cap. On the walls were posters of wanted men and women – Yakuzas, communist terrorists, prison shots in black-and-white. There were coloured advertisements showing the work of the police: directing traffic, holding children's hands, helping old ladies across the street.

For weeks now we had been passing this building, and we had assumed that it was always manned. It had a glass-panelled front with a commanding view of the district. Sometimes we would make detours in order to avoid it. Now we realised it must normally be empty.

Some time ago, Pungay had done something which now turned out to be very useful. He had written to his wife, asking for a photograph of herself with assorted children of different heights. This emerged when we were made to turn out our pockets, and Pungay – who was normally so shy of speaking Nihonggo that I had to order his meals for him – immediately went into a routine.

'Look, sacho,' he said, 'this is my wife. My children. Four. Please, please. They will suffer.'

I'd known this was coming. If there was a standard phrase-book for illegal workers, this would be in it. For myself, although I was pretending to know very little Japanese, I took care to use as many forms of apology as I could fit in.

The policeman showed no sign of melting at the photograph. 'Don't you know,' he said, 'that what you're doing is against the law. It's bad.'

'Gommennasai,' I said.

'Sumimasen,' said Pungay. And we bowed our heads. By now we had a new routine. Every time I said Gommennasai, Pungay would say Sumimasen, and if I said Sumimasen, he would say Gommennasai. I kicked him under the table. We were sounding ridiculous.

The policeman picked up the phone and dialled Yokohama Immigration. As he relayed the facts of our case, Pungay buried his face in his arms and began to snuffle. I pressed my foot on his and suppressed a giggle. Our feet began a vigorous conversation. The policeman dialled again, and then again. He dialled seven numbers but without success. It was five o'clock. They were too busy to attend to us. Pungay kept snuffling.

Finally he said, 'Tomorrow, come back here and bring your passports. If you don't,' he pointed to his empty holster, 'I will – like this.' He aimed an imaginary gun at us. 'Bang! Bang!'

We sprang to our feet. '*Arigatou gozaimasu, sacho-san!*' we exclaimed simultaneously, and bowed lavishly, and fled from the office and out of sight, clenching our teeth to suppress our giggles.

17

The Second America

IN THE END, it was fear that made me surrender. It wasn't fear of the police or the immigration agents, and it wasn't the danger of the daily work. It was the routine and the discipline that I began to dread, the way it stretched out ahead, day after day: if not stevedoring – construction work, if not construction work – stevedoring. I hated the helmets and the safety shoes. I hated the way the sachos ordered us around. I hated counting up the daily humiliations of the Standing Men – and not only our humiliations as Filipinos, but those of our Japanese colleagues. And I hated the uncertainty. Arrest would be one thing – if you knew it was going to come. But I didn't want someone grabbing me by the waistband while I was taking a pee. Not to be able to pack and say goodbye to my friends, to be whisked off unceremoniously into detention, even an hour in prison would be a dreadful humiliation.

Humiliation is the key. The Japanese police do not have a reputation for violence in their handling of illegal immigrants. We didn't expect to be beaten up in the cells, or to be at the mercy of corrupt officers such as we have back home. If I was told that I had to spend the night in Manila City Jail, I would be utterly, physically terrified, and I would do anything in my power to bribe my way out. The Japanese police were not saints. I'd heard of one man bribing his way out of a patrol car, and of a girl who had given sexual favours in order to avoid arrest. If you put up a violent resistance you could expect to be punched around a bit. But this was not what you feared when you surrendered.

All my friends said that if I gave myself up I should expect to be detained at least overnight. I dreaded the shame involved in this, but there was no way out. I needed to get my papers in order again, and the only way to do this was to give yourself up.

For a while I delayed, waiting for the first snow-fall. Filipinos are crazy about the snow. The oji-chans used to tease us about this, saying that the snow was the best *o-miyage*, souvenir, we could take home. But it was true that I wanted to see my fellow-countrymen working in the snow, and to photograph them. I wanted to play in it myself, as I had the previous winter when I was a student. But February came, and still no snow, and I decided I could wait no longer.

I had been working now for almost a year, and had saved nearly ¥150,000 – about two weeks' wages. I had a stills camera and a secondhand Video-8 camera, and a share in some other film equipment that Wilson, Manny and I had bought. I had a room full of junk – notebooks, poems, letters, clippings and souvenirs. In comparison with Wilson, Manny and Jeff, I had not done very well – about $1000 to take home, whereas they had been remitting that much per month. But photography is expensive and I had the makings of a video documentary.

And besides, my friends were in the first league of the savers. There were plenty of others like them, but they were still a minority among the people I knew. Most of the people in my building lived from day to day. If they had come to Japan with the common illusion that they would save enough for a house, or some land, or a small shop, or a jeepney, that ambition hadn't lasted. The money had not found its way home, and never would. It was mostly in circulation in Yokohama.

If it had not been splashed out on a good time, it had gone on cheap status symbols – the home appliances, the enormous televisions and sound systems, video players and cameras, the gold jewellery – things which would be important back home but which wouldn't in the long term have any effect on your standard of living.

Indeed, a brief period of comparative wealth could

make things more difficult for the future. The greater the regular remittance home, the greater the family demands – the demands of the in-laws, the brothers, the cousins, the long-lost friends and remote relatives. A man would come home to find himself responsible for the well-being of a whole clan, and it would be hard to scale down the expenditure.

Edgardo, for instance, was the most industrious of the lot. He had no vices, and he lived on noodles to save money. He used to work on Sundays and holidays, and he set himself the target of remitting $2000 a month. After two years he went home. He now owned two passenger jeepneys, and an extravagantly refurbished house with a small shop attached. He had two sophisticated electronic cameras, a fancy Video-8, everything. By any standards, he was well ahead of the game.

Barely a month after his arrival, he was selling all his cameras and his jeepneys and was applying to the Japanese Embassy under an assumed name, together with several of his mates from Kotobuki. The income from the jeepneys and the shop couldn't begin to support the new life style of his children. There were only two of them, and the fact that they were both in college shouldn't have meant such a large expenditure. A peasant with two hectares of riceland should be able to put his children through college, providing the family continues to live like peasants.

Edgardo lived in Tondo, near the famous slum. His house had become the meeting-place for all his children's friends, and his children by now were thoroughly spoiled. They were dedicated shoppers and party-goers. The jeepneys were at the disposal of the children, who liked organising picnics in far-flung places. The daughter had become a local beauty queen, more through money than any natural talent. The son, at seventeen, had got a girl pregnant and had married her. Neither father nor son fancied the life of a jeepney driver. Indeed the son's only ambition was to accompany his father to Japan. I said to Edgardo, 'But he's too young. You think he can carry a box of bananas?' Edgardo said, 'I want him to experience what I've experienced. Let him suffer also.'

In Japan, Edgardo had had a reputation for tight-fistedness, and at the worksite he loved to flick through his money during break. All his talent was for living cheaply, in a room smaller than mine, which he even shared. Back in Manila, he was incompetent at being rich, and his son had inherited that incompetence. He was a miserable, skinny boy. I guessed from his eyes that he was on drugs. His young wife looked equally miserable, with a plain face and terrible teeth. Edgardo had told his son that, now he was to become a father, he would have to face his responsibilities. This, the son thought, he was prepared to do. But when I looked at him I could see that his future in Koto was bleak. The sachos wouldn't hire him, and if they did he wouldn't stand the pace.

I tried to argue with Edgardo, and to point out that he was already a lucky man, with no reason to return to the living conditions in Japan. But although he liked being told he was a rich man, he had already made calculations: it would take months to prepare his new papers, and the last of his savings were already earmarked for the necessary bribes. Besides, although he complained about the way his kids had behaved, there was a side of him that was proud of the fact they had money to burn. In Tondo! It is always the case that children who have parents in Saudi or Japan or anywhere abroad become more popular with their classmates.

Status is the key. When I was going to high school, I used to take a lunch that consisted of one egg, rice, two tomatoes and salt. I was envied by my friends in the barrio because I was going to the protestant, private school. To earn the fare to school, my brother and I would sell vegetables in the market on Sunday. I didn't like my classmates, especially the girls, to see me doing this, but we didn't consider this a particular hardship.

Today, the difference between rich and poor in the barrio is much more visible. The *baon*, the child's allowance of money or food, is the first great divider within the school: can you afford Coke and bread in the break? Can you even take your lunch at one of the market restaurants? If so, in terms of barrio life, that means you have a relative abroad. The other status symbols follow in order of expense and prestige: the shirt with the brand name, the Levis, the athletic shoes, the motorcycle and the . . . piano lessons! Piano lessons have a particular significance: they imply that you are not planting rice or weeding, and that you don't intend to do so either.

Sundays in the barrio are much like Sundays in Kotobuki. The church is the place where the women and children can display their new wealth, and *driving* to church – even if it's only a hundred yards away – is particularly desirable. White clothes for the children, high heels, a hair-do and a veil for the mother – the chic, devout look. Then the newly wealthy families begin to find occasions to invite the priest to celebrate mass at home: thanksgiving for a graduation, school honours, an eighteenth birthday début. Unfamiliar excuses for parties are found – Mother's day, Father's day, Valentine's day . . . The houses of the newly rich draw crowds of children in the evening, with their videos and enormous TVs. The local politicians and dignitaries are drawn in, to partake and admire, and this becomes a passport to real status, and even power.

Often in the past, people have written about Filipino migrant workers as if the issue was one of simple economic need. The issue is economic, but it is not simple. It is not the case that a man faces starvation in Negros and so decides to go to Kotobuki. If he was facing starvation in Negros, he wouldn't begin to be able to think of going abroad. It is only when you have some cash in hand or the ability to raise a loan that you can start thinking in those terms.

Viewed in the Japanese context, the Standing Man, waiting to greet the sacho on the Kotobuki sidewalk, is a member of an underclass. Obliged to live illegally, he has no say over his working conditions; the only certainty in his life comes at the end of the day, when he can see whether he had work that day and what he got paid for it. But viewed from the perspective of the barrio, this same man is a member of a privileged class. He is, we would say, blessed. When he returns to the barrio, people will gather around him, and when he speaks of his life in Japan it will be with pride. The barrio will not be told of his sufferings and humiliations. It will hear of the wonders of the push-button world, of the Bullet Train, the skyscrapers and Tokyo Disneyland. In the stories with which he regales his *barkadas*, his mates, this returning hero will feature as a sexual adventurer, and a wise guy, cunningly outwitting the Japanese, despite all their technological prowess. But even if he told the truth about the life he had been living, he would not succeed in discouraging people from following his example.

Now a man may sincerely believe that he is working in Japan in order to amass some finite amount of capital to secure his future back home, but if you look at what actually happens it seems inevitable that he will be caught in a spiral of increased expectations. The richer you are in the Philippines, the more likely you are to go abroad and to settle there for good.

It was contact with America, or the idea of America, that fostered in the Philippines the deep pessimism about the Philippines that affects every level of society. Before this century, under Spanish colonial rule, only a tiny élite could have been infected by the desire to go to Spain. A few of their descendants still maintain contact, and continue to speak Spanish at home – but this happens only in a few exclusive families. The American culture, on the other hand, is pervasive.

It is particularly debilitating among the middle class. A rich family in the barrio, with land, income from tenants, various small business interests such as rice dealing, a shop, and money-lending – a family well supplied with poor relatives who do the household work in return for their modest keep – will nevertheless dream of decamping to the States. Their children are educated to the point where they could enter the professions. But then the great opportunity arises. A relative in California petitions on their behalf, and off they go, to become apple-pickers, waiters, garbage collectors, baby-sitters.

All their life they have been prepared for this great moment. They have been brought up to call their parents Daddy and Mommy. The language spoken around the house is an absurd mixture of native dialect, Pilipino and as much English as comes to hand. A girl will be told: 'Study to be a nurse, because one day you will go to America.' Boys will be pushed in the direction of engineering because of its international usefulness. The idea of the inferiority of everything Filipino is deeply inculcated.

The target countries for those who wish to make their fortunes abroad are divided into two sharply distinct categories: the welcomers and the stonewallers. America leads the first category, along with Canada and Australia, as being places where you would expect to settle down. The Middle East, Hong Kong and Japan hold out no such illusions. You stay in Saudi for just as long as you can stand it, in Japan for as long as you can wangle it.

There is no Japanese Dream, and yet Japan, for the Filipino, has become a second America. There is no Statue of Liberty in Yokohama – why should there be? A statue of the Yen would be more appropriate. We do not dream of becoming Japanese citizens – even for the brides who achieve this, it is a secondary consideration. We do not imagine that we will settle there for ever. We know that we will not be accepted, and anyway we cannot imagine submitting to the extreme discipline of Japanese life. Still, more and more, we see Japan as part of our future.

The Japanese are now the largest investors and

aid donors to the Philippines. They are our wealthiest tourists. More and more Filipinos are studying Nihonggo, in new language schools and on television. Even the beggars and street-vendors of Manila have developed a Japanese patter. As the Filipino underground grows in Japan, so the Japanese underground takes hold in Manila, Cebu, Baguio, Davao. Indeed, they are the same underground, catering for needs that the legitimate channels do not meet.

But so many different needs are involved. Japan needs more day-labourers than it admits. The salaryman needs a night out with an exotic beauty. Edgardo would find he needed to return to Koto because he had embarked on the pursuit of status. Margie needed a network of docile men – customers and lovers – to support her existence.

Kazuo had needed an obliging subject for a photo-essay, whom he would follow from the Philippines to Japan, and he held out the prospect of my earning real money for the first time. I needed to do something with my life. I wanted to get away from the Left, with its endless theoretical talk of exploited, oppressed masses. I wanted to experience the reality of labour, and if I made a bit of money thereby, so much the better.

A year later, I no longer needed to find out if I could survive in such a world. I'd answered that question. I could survive, but not for ever. I could well believe that if it had been America I could have been lured into staying on for ever. But not in this humiliating world of hide and seek. The mere sight of my helmet filled me with nausea and dread.

18

I Surrender

I TOLD MAYUMI of my plan. If I was to surrender, I needed her moral support and if I was put in jail, I wanted her to inform my friends. I dreaded what might happen, but I knew it was better to surrender than get caught. Friday would be the best day to turn yourself in – the busiest time of the week, when formalities tend to get disregarded, and the salarymen are tired, looking forward to an evening in the bar. I might be asked fewer questions and would get away with fewer lies.

As news of my impending surrender spread, however, I received two less welcome offers of support. Akihiro was keen to record the events: for him I was material, as I had been for Kazuo, the sample migrant worker in the sample surrender. And then there was Saburo, from the Japanese day-labourers' union, who was keen that my rights be respected. I was grateful, but dismayed at their attention. I didn't want to arrive with a delegation. My view was – the more I played dumb, the less I seemed to know about my rights (whatever they might be), the more lenient the authorities would be.

Friday came, and the four of us took breakfast in a fancy restaurant called Dennis. Each dish on the menu was marked with its calorie equivalent. My order came to 983 calories precisely, and during the walk to the immigration office I turned over in my mind the significance of the number. Nine, I thought, was the maximum number of days I would spend in jail. Eight would be the reduced sentence if I managed to get the interrogator to smile just once. Three, a lucky number, a biblical number, referred to the questions I would have to answer satisfactorily. I began to shiver at the thought of meeting Mr Igme.

His office is at the top of an eight-storey building, and we waited for the *erebeta* amid a throng of Filipinas, dressed to kill, with emphatic tights, high heels or high-cut Reeboks, plenty of gold and glamorous dark glasses in the gloom. Their papa-san was also in a kind of uniform, with the short curled hair, dark glasses and bulging clutchbag of the Yakuza.

I had expected something more threatening, an individual cell with a single interrogator. But the room marked Enforcement Division was a large open-plan office, without any security guards, guns or uniforms – none of the impedimenta you would have found in the Philippines. There was nothing to suggest that clients passed from this office into anything like a jail. The simple blue jackets of the immigration men, draped over the backs of their chairs, were the same as those worn by post office employees and other civil servants. The atmosphere was the same as that of any office anywhere in Japan.

And this was the building that my fellow workers would sometimes point out from the coach, on the way back from the docks, saying, 'Hey, Tisoy, if you're caught, that's where you'll go. That's the office of the Mig-mig. You'll rot in there.' I'd seen the police enough times, but I'd never seen the Mig-mig – or never knowingly. That was one of the things that scared us about them – we didn't know what they looked like. A Filipino Mig-mig would have a distinct notorious look: the pot belly, the macho swagger, the gun in the clutchbag – the look that says: I am here to be bribed. But those like Zaldy who had had a brush with the Mig-mig here, and had escaped, were often surprised at how young they were, and how slightly built. Now I could see, glancing round the room, that the thing about the Mig-mig was that they didn't *have* a look. Everything about the Enforcement Division was bafflingly normal.

I had been determined not to reveal my address, not to put my fellow workers in jeopardy. I came on like an illiterate, claiming not to know where I lived, beyond the vague description, Kotobuki. The interrogator very kindly took this act at face value. He produced, and laid out under my nose, a highly detailed map of the neighbourhood. Then, beginning with the tall Labour Building, he pointed out all the landmarks of Koto. He knew everything! Right down to the position of the 24-hour convenience shop which abutted our building. And when I finally pointed to the building, he immediately knew its name.

I was shocked. Even though I had always suspected that we lived in Koto on sufferance, I hadn't fully appreciated that when we thought we were hiding we were doing no such thing. All our efforts to live invisibly were nothing more than a charade in which the workers, the recruiters, the Mig-mig and the police all played their part. We lived in hiding. They pretended not to see us. When public opinion demanded, they made a token raid. For the rest of the time, we were a necessary evil. We thought we were so clever. We thought we knew the ropes. *Whom did we think we were kidding?*

I wasn't arrested or detained. Quite the contrary – I was told to go out and take some lunch at midday, and then the weekend intervened before the whole legal process could be completed. I went back to work on the Saturday, to a building-site which I had known since it was a wooded hill, and which was now an almost finished block of flats. We'd been involved at every stage. We cleared the ground, we dug the foundations, now we were erecting scaffolding so that the building could be painted. It gave me a hidden pleasure, a secret delight, to see the thing so near completion. In my mind, I laid a cornerstone with the inscription: 'The apartment complex rose with the aid of illegal foreign labour.'

I climbed the scaffolding with a light heart. The work was dangerous in its way, but I no longer felt scared. It didn't feel like work – it felt like gymnastics, swinging around on the parallel bars. The *racheto*, the ratchet wrench, made a satisfying clicking sound which could be turned into music, and because we were at the back of the building, out of sight, and it was Saturday and the sacho wasn't around, we were able to sing our Filipino songs. We sang love songs, ballads – anything that came to mind, filling in the lines we'd forgotten with nonsense. Ramon stood below, tossing up the clamps. Pungay and I were like a circus double act. Ramon had a fire going, and we took as many breaks as we wanted. I set my camera to automatic, for souvenir snaps.

I felt free and I felt I'd *won* – won in the sense of Kotobuki slang. If you don't find work, we say you've lost, that day. If you're cheated on your pay, if you don't get overtime, you've lost. You've won if you've been able to remit money. I'd won, in the sense that, although I'd got a scar on the chest, I still had the use of all my limbs. Overall, I hadn't been cheated too badly, and I had money and possessions, something to show for it all. Although I'd 'played the piano' (had my fingerprints taken), which was humiliating, and had been photographed like a common criminal, holding name and number on a blackboard, I hadn't been put in jail. I would not be escorted out of the country by the police.

People would say to me, 'Hey, Tisoy, why are you going now? You've got a good job. There are still millions of yen for the grabbing. You've already won – you even have a *japonesa*!'

It's true that I was lucky. There was Mayumi. But we had already agreed to meet again in the Philippines after her graduation. And Mr Igme informed me, as he handed me my completed papers, that I would be free to return to Japan in a year's time. And I knew that if I *did* return, it would be because of her. I was through with the underground. I wasn't through with Japan.

Japalog Dictionary

THE FILIPINO LANGUAGE, Pilipino or Tagalog, is rich in foreign borrowings, mostly from Spanish or English. Nouns may survive in recognisable form: *krismas* for Christmas. Or they may be turned into verbs by a complicated set of grammatical rules involving suffixes, reduplications and infixes (the insertion of syllables within the root word). *Krinismasan*, for instance, means 'to give for Christmas'; *magkikrismas ako sa probinsya* means 'I will spend Christmas in the province'.

Because most people in the Philippines grow up speaking their regional language or dialect, learning Pilipino second and English third, the languages inevitably get mixed up. When I talk with my brother, we may move from Ilokano to Pilipino to English and back in the course of a few sentences. In the showbiz language of Manila, Taglish, English and Filipino phrases co-exist within a single sentence. An

American accent is affected throughout. Among the upper classes you will find Engalog-speakers, whose English is better than their Tagalog, as well as a very few homes in which Spanish is used exclusively.

Given our tendency to mix, borrow and invent linguistically, it is not surprising to find that Koto has its own special slang, including Japanese loan-words, Japalog conjugations, surviving slang from World War II and the argot of the Manila under-world.

Japalog delights in mimicking the sounds of Japan-ese words, with rhymed variations and flights of nonsense using strings of brandnames. Whereas the showbiz set in Manila imitate American accents because they admire American style, mimicry in Koto is all to do with mockery. If you saw two Filipinos in Manila kissing each other as a greeting, that would mean they were advertising their Westernisation. It would strike us as very pretentious. If on the other hand they bowed, that would mean they had been in Japan, and it would be a joke. We do not *emulate* the Japanese. Other gestures imitated in Koto include the raised thumb to indicate a man, and the little finger for a woman. The index finger drawn diagonally across the upper cheek means a Yakuza. A Filipino when referring to himself might point to his heart. A Japanese will tap his nose with his forefinger. It would be impossible for us to do that seriously.

Here is a short dictionary of usage in Koto.

Aishiteru (Jap.) 'I love you'. Used lavishly and light-heartedly by Filipinos, both in flirtations and as an answer to an insult. (See under *bakkero*).

Ano sa, watashiwa anatawa nakakatawa ka! The ungrammatical sentence, beginning in Japanese, is designed to attract the attention of the sacho ('It seems ... I ... you ... ') before turning into Tagalog on the last two words, which mean 'You're funny'.

Arigato singkamas (Jap. & Pil.) 'Thank you turnips' – in which the second word has been substituted for *gozaimasu*, 'Thank you very much'.

Atama (Jap.) 'Head'. In Koto slang, penis.

Baka 'Fool' in Japanese and 'cow' in Pilipino. If the sacho calls you *baka* you reply in Japanese *Oishi!* (delicious).

Bakkero or *Kunnero* Two common forms of Japanese insult, intensifying *baka*. Used between friends, may be affectionate. From sacho to worker, usually an insult. You reply in Japanese *Aishiteru!* (q.v.) *Binakkero kami buong araw* – We were insulted the whole day (Japalog).

Banana 'Dock work', covering unloading of oranges, grapefruit, anything in boxes, but not frozen goods. See under *Freezer*.

Bata (Pil.) 'Child'. Macho slang for girlfriend.

-chan Intimate form of honorific *-san*. Between Filipino friends, a memory of a common past in Japan.

Daijabou (Jap.) 'OK'.

Dare? 'Who?' Aggressive answer to knock on door. (See Ch. 1).

Denwa (Jap.) 'Telephone'. *Homsik na homsik ako. Magdedenwa ako sa 'pinas.* I'm terribly homesick. I'm going to telephone to the Philippines.

Dokata (Jap.) 'Labourer', 'navvy'. *Ang yabang-yabang mo na ngayon. Dokata-boy ka lang noon.* You are so arrogant now. But before you were just a dokata-boy.

Domo shinkansen (Jap.) 'Thank you bullet-train.' As opposed to *Domo summimasen* thank you very much.

Freezer Covers work unloading frozen goods from ships; highly paid but unpopular work. *Kung walang banana, mag-freezer na lang tayo.* If there's no banana (q.v.), let's just do freezer (work).

Gemba (Jap.) 'Worksite'. *Ni-reyd kami sa gemba.* We were raided at the worksite.

Genki ka? (Jap.) 'Are you OK?' Grammatically similar to Pilipino, the expression is much used in mockery of someone who has had, for instance, a box of bananas fall on his head. The reply would be *Bakkero* (q.v.).

Gokkoro sama (Jap.) 'Thank you very much', (at the end of the day, for a job well done). The reply, delivered with mock politeness and a voice trailing away, is: *Ang sama-sama ng mukha mo* – you have a very ugly face.

Gomi (Jap.) 'Rubbish, garbage'. (n. or v.) In Koto

slang, this is always the desirable rubbish. *Punong-puno ng gomi ang kwarto ni Eddie – rays kuker, tibi at iba pa.* Eddie's room is full of rubbish – rice cooker, TV – everything. *Nakagomi ako ng 'sang-kartong bomba komiks.* I gomi-ed a box of porno mags.

Gomennasai (Jap.) 'I'm sorry'. (v.) *Mahirap mag-gomennasai ang mga siga ng Koto.* It's difficult for the (Filipino) bullies of Koto to apologise.

Hai (Jap.) 'Yes'. Used subversively, as in *Hai, wakarimasen.* Yes, I do not understand. Also in numerous meaningless rhymes.

Hapon (Pil.) 'Japanese'. In left-wing Manila slang this means police or military agent (from WWII usage). In Kotobuki the meaning is neutral.

Haponesa (Pil.) 'Japanese woman'. WWII slang for prostitute. In Kotobuki, neutral. Abbr. *'nesa. Hanep si Tisoy, nakabata ng 'nesa.* Lucky Tisoy! He's got a Japanese girlfriend.

Ichi-nichi (Jap.) Lit. 'One-day'. 'Day-labourer'. *Ang buhay namin sa Koto ay ichi-nichi – minsan malas, minsan suwerte.* Our life in Koto is lived on a day-to-day basis – sometimes unlucky, sometimes lucky.

Igme (Pil.) Abbr. of *Igmedio.* Nickname for immigration agent. *Ingat sa Igme.* Watch out for the immigration people.

Ippuku (Jap.) Break in work for one cigarette. Commonly used in sexual context.

Jangkenpo Scissors, paper, stone. (See Ch.12).

Kaitai (Jap.) 'Demolition'. (n. or v.) *Tignan mo siya, mukhang kaitai na.* Look at him, he's got a face like a demolition site.

Kaitai-boy 'Demolition-worker'.

Karaoke (Jap.) Sing-along bar. In Koto slang, blow-job.

Kawaii (Jap.) 'Pretty'. In Koto slang, *Kawaiiko-chan!* – manner of addressing pretty girl on street, often followed by (vul. Pil.) *Iyyot Ta!* Let's fuck.

Koibito (Jap.) 'Girlfriend' or 'boyfriend'.

Kokoro (Jap.) 'Heart'. As in (Japalog) *Kokoro kara mahal kita.* From the bottom of my heart I love you.

Koto Abbr. *Kotobuki. Ang Koto ay paraiso, ang Koto ay langit.* Koto is paradise, Koto is heaven.

Kulot (Pil.) 'Crinkly hair'. Yakuza member.

Kubi (Jap.) 'Fired'. *Kinubi sila dahil sa isang pinya.* They were fired for one pineapple.

Lak-lak (Pil.) Lit. 'to scratch the skin'. *Walang banana ngayon. Mag-laklak na lang tayo.* There's no banana (dock-work) today. Let's drink cough syrup instead.

Lapad (Pil.) 'Broad', 'a broad one'. Refers to a ¥10,000 bill.

Lespu Inversion of (Pil.) *pulis.* 'Police'. The word *pulis* is always avoided.

Mama-san In Koto slang means 'landlady', else-where 'brothel madame'.

Manku, o-manku (Jap.) 'Vagina'. *Mangkok* (Pil.) means a bowl for food. A common pun.

May-palong (Pil.) 'Having a cock's comb', refers to a police patrol car with its flashing light.

Mig-mig (Koto sl.) Immigration agent. *Nang dahil sa San Mig, nahuli siya ng Mig-mig.* Because of San Miguel (beer), he was arrested by the immigration.

Mise, o-mise (Jap.) Bar. *Nasa gemba ang hirap, nasa mise ang sarap.* Hardship at the jobsite, pleasure in the bar. (Koto proverb).

Nani (Jap.) 'What?' Conveniently replaces (Pil.) *Ano* in conversations between friends who have been in Japan.

Ne (Jap.) Common exclamation, imitated, as in *ne, ni, no, nu* (like a child learning how to read).

Odori From Odori Park, (n. or v.), referring to flea market in Yokohama or elsewhere. *Tara sa Tokyo. May Odori doon.* Let's go to Tokyo. There's an Odori there. *Odori-boy*, frequenter of flea market. *Akala mo kung pumorma! Odori-boy lang pala.* Comes on as if he's somebody. But he's just an Odori-boy.

O-furo (Jap.) 'Public bath'. (n. or v.) *Kahit ang mga latak ng Koto ay nag-oopuro.* Even the dregs of Koto go to the bath-house.

O-hayo (Jap.) 'Good morning'. *Nag-ohayo ka na ba?* Have you greeted (the recruiter) yet?

Oji-san or *Oji-chan* (Jap.) 'Old Man'. Two polite ways of referring to your Japanese fellow labourers, who would normally be older than you.

Papa-san In Koto slang is used (a) as an affectionate address for an *Oji-chan* (q.v.) (b) to denote a landlord affectionately, where applicable. Outside Koto and in the Philippines, pimp or brothel manager.

Parak Koto and Manila underworld slang for police. The implication is always hostile.

Pinagpala (Pil.) Either 'blessed' or 'made to use the spade'. A common pun.

Pinay (Pil.) Common abbr. for a Filipina.

Pinkoro (Jap.) 'Filipino'. Offensive, equivalent of Chongko (Korean). Use provokes powerful verbal or physical response.

Pinoy (Pil.) Common abbr. for a Filipino.

Ponjaps Inversion of Japanese (see *Lespu*). In Manila left-wing slang, it means an agent (see *Hapon*). In Koto, merely a diplomatic disguise of the word.

Putol (Pil.) 'Cut finger', referring to a lower-ranking Yakuza member.

Sacho (from Jap. *Shacho*) 'Boss', recruiter, any Japanese man of whom a Filipino is asking a favour.

Sakang (Pil.) 'Bow-legged', WWII slang for Japanese. Derogatory.

Sayonara (Jap.) 'Farewell'. Used on occasions of formal leave-taking by the Japanese, but by Filipinos as a colloquial everyday goodbye.

Shigoto (Jap.) 'Job'. The first sentence every Filipino learns is *Ohayo gozaimasu*, good morning sir; the second is *Shigoto arimasu ka?* Do you have a job (to offer)? Also used in a sexual context, as in *Shishigotohin ko ang aking asawa*, I am going to *shigoto* my lover.

Shoji (Jap.) 'Cleaning job'. *Magsosoji muna ako*, I am going to clean (my room).

Shokai (Jap.) 'Introduction'. *Magkano ang shokai-fee mo?* How much is your introduction fee? (for an illegal job).

So-so-so (Jap.) 'Yes, yes, yes.' *So-so* (Pil.) means breast. Common pun.

Sungki (Pil.) 'Overlapping teeth'. A Japanese girl.

Sungkit (Pil.) 'To hook'. In Koto, refers to the act of cheating the laundry machine, the drier or the coin-operated gas stove. A *Sungkit-boy* such as Zaldy (Ch. 15) might fix a machine for you in return for a can of juice.

Supot (Pil.) 'Uncircumcised'. Derogatory slang for Japanese. In the Philippines, *supot* means coward, effeminate, not yet a man.

Tachimbo (Jap.) 'Standing Man'. In Koto, it means the 'day-labourers' standing on the corners every morning waiting for a job.

Tegami (Jap.) 'Letter'. *May tegami ako mula sa aking waswit.* I have a letter from my sweetheart (*waswit*, being a Manila corruption of sweetheart).

Toka (Jap.) 'The tenth'. The system of being paid on the tenth day.

Untug-tuhod (Pil.) 'Knock-knees'. Derogatory for Japanese.

Yak-yak (Pil.)   Member of Yakuza gang.

Yukuza (Pil.)   'Henpecked husband'. From *yuku sa asawa*, bow to the wife.

Afterword

WE KNOW FROM many personal accounts what it is like to be a Japanese abroad. To be sure, the more interesting of these accounts stress the personal rather than the Japanese. The experiences, ranging from bewildered reactions of samurai arriving in Victorian San Francisco to hip Sixties writers attending, notebook in hand, wife-swapping parties in the same place a century later, are too varied to be able to speak of a typical Japanese abroad. Obviously the story of a poor Japanese woman shanghaied in Yokohama in 1928 to work the brothels of South-east Asia will have little, if anything, in common with the account of a Tokyo University academic doing research at Harvard.

Nonetheless, from the mosaic of vastly different stories of Japanese encounters with foreigners certain tendencies might be discerned. To start with, there is the Japanese penchant for ranks and categories. There is, for example, a racial ranking system. On top of the pyramid is the white race, followed by the Chinese races, and under them the South-east Asians, then the Arabs, the Indians and finally, way down at the bottom of the pile, those of African descent. As in most places, the ranking goes up and down according to skin-colour. But this rather crude list is subject to exceptions and variations. Indians are sometimes respected more than say, the South-east Asians, because of their ancient civilisation. The Koreans, though part of the same stock as the Japanese themselves, frequently are despised more than any other nationality. And the whites, though at the racial pinnacle, are sometimes regarded with disdain for being crude, arrogant and ill-bred.

Racial hierarchy, as the Korean example shows, is further complicated by national prejudices. These tend to follow closely the political and economic fortunes of the countries concerned. The stereotypes are not hard to guess: Germans are industrious and disciplined, thus wholly admirable, rather like the Japanese themselves; the British are gentlemen, but lazy, sloppy and increasingly powerless; the French are cultured but arrogant, the Americans frank but crude, the Swiss peaceful, and so on. In Asia, the Indians and Chinese are pretty hopeless now, but were great once; the Thais are graceful; the Malays lazy and the Filipinos, well . . . perhaps the attitude to them was illustrated crassly but honestly in a popular magazine – I think it was the Japanese edition of

Playboy – which ran a photo story not so long after People Power toppled Ferdinand Marcos. The photographs showed a couple of naked dark-skinned girls, one of whom had her arms wrapped round a fierce-looking guerilla fighter, while the other was fondling a machine-gun. Rough sex indeed.

Speaking of sex, blacks, though at the bottom of the racial hierarchy, score highly with some Japanese women, not only for the usual reasons – rhythm, physical prowess and all that jazz – but also because they appeal to a maternal desire to nurture and protect. Blacks are *kawaiso*, literally to be pitied. There may even be an element of solidarity here, since the social position of Japanese women is in many ways kawaiso. The desire to be taken care of, in the case of many Japanese women, is expressed in a sometimes cloying cuteness. When Americans protested about the Japanese liking for little black Sambos and Golliwog dolls, the Japanese were genuinely bewildered. What could possibly be so offensive about a Golliwog? Wasn't he cute and cuddly? Indeed a bit like a Japanese girl?

Japanese prejudices are often so transparent, they seem almost innocent. When I was a student in Tokyo in the 1970s, and went round the estate agents in search of a flat, it was not at all uncommon to be the uncomfortable witness of the following telephone dialogue between agent and potential landlord:

> Agent: We have a single person here looking for a flat . . .
>
> Landlord: Yes?
>
> Agent: A student . . .
>
> Landlord: Yes?
>
> Agent: Well, actually, to tell you the truth, he is a foreigner, but he speaks Japanese, and he's not a South-east Asian or anything of that sort . . .
>
> Landlord: I see . . .
>
> Agent: No, no, not Chinese or Korean either, no, rest assured, he's white, a white foreigner . . .

And so on, until it became quite clear that I wouldn't get on with this landlord, however much he might be mollified by my white skin.

We also know what it's like for a white foreigner to live in Japan. There are accounts starting with the Dutch traders stuck on a tiny island off Nagasaki in the seventeenth century. Apart from specialised prostitutes and visiting functionaries, these men hardly ever saw a Japanese, for their hosts did not approve of contact beyond the absolute minimum necessary for trade.

Things have changed of course. Even though there is still a large number of Westerners – bankers, businessmen, diplomats and the like – whose contacts with the Japanese are restricted to their professional duties, many have gone beyond that. There are the romantics, following in the footsteps of Lefcadio Hearn, who live in wooden houses, preferably in Kyoto, lighting joss-sticks and wearing a kimono around the house. There are those with a more Spartan taste who go in for Zen. Others enter the world of fashion, theatre, or film. Many, by living in Japan, become what the French call *tatamisé*, too used to the smell of straw mats to be comfortable anywhere else again. Some flee back to their native countries in horror. Japan leaves few foreigners indifferent. Perhaps it would be most accurate to say that the majority of Western foreigners in Japan both love and hate the country, depending on the time of day.

The happiest Westerners in Japan are usually those who expect least of it. The unhappiest are undoubtedly those who wish to, as it were, become Japanese, in the way one becomes an American, or an Anglophile might attempt to become an Englishman. This is a mistake. Japanese can be generous and courteous hosts, even to those who after many years of residence hardly any longer qualify as guests. But a guest, in Japanese eyes, always remains a guest.

Foreigners are special in Japan and there are some who like being special, who enjoy being asked about the 'blue-eyed point of view' on anything from the prospects of world peace to the taste of raw tuna. Being special means being subject to discrimination. Not always in a negative way. One is different, so one is not only licensed to behave differently from

Japanese, one is expected to do so. Westerners who resent this, who wish to blend in and be treated like everybody else, tire of being asked about the blue-eyed point of view, or being told how the Westerner is king in Japan, or how skilfully one uses chopsticks. Such foreigners are well advised to leave.

But at any rate, we know from many books, articles and whatnot how these Westerners feel about Japan. The same is true of the romantics, the enthusiasts, the casual travellers, the experts, the get-rich-quick merchants, and so on and so forth. Much less is known, at least in European languages, about the feelings of other Asians *vis-à-vis* Japan. Most people are aware of the fact, it is true, that the Koreans love Japan about as much as the Irish love England. One cannot blame them for this, since they were not only treated brutally during the first half of this century, but they almost lost their right to be Koreans at all. During the last stage of Japanese occupation Japanese became the mandatory language in Korean schools and people were forced to adopt Japanese names.

That Chinese and South-east Asians still have more vivid memories of the Japanese war of conquest than many Japanese would like is an equally understandable and well publicised fact. But much of this is at the level of popular prejudice, manipulated by governments and the press, often, it must be said, with considerable assistance from tactless Japanese officials.

What we do not know much about – and this is where Rey Ventura's book is so important – is how other Asians actually feel about living in Japan. Unlike Westerners, they are rarely privileged guests. There are few cultural romantics amongst them. I have never heard of a Filipino, say, who walked around his wooden house in Kyoto in a kimono thinking of traditional woodcuts. Few Thais or Malaysians attend Kabuki performances, or try their hand at ink painting. And rarely, if ever, does one see Asians on television panels offering 'the brown-eyed point of view' on peace or raw tuna. I think it is fair to say that most Asians come to Japan, not because it is charming, but because it is rich and technologically advanced. Asians are in Japan to make money or to study, mostly useful things, like engineering, medicine or accounting.

The ones making money are, I think, the more interesting: the immigrant workers, often living outside the law, the grifters and bargirls and construction gangs; the Bangladeshi waiters and Chinese cooks, the Taiwanese strippers and Iranian day-labourers. These people, whether Japanese officials like it or not, are changing Japan for ever. They also have an interesting perspective on Japanese society that few outsiders, or even Japanese themselves are likely to share; for they are thrown into the deep end, with the dregs of the economic miracle: the petty criminals and general losers, whose lives perhaps tell us more about contemporary Japan than those of the main-stream salarymen who keep the miracle going. As is apparent from Ventura's fascinating encounters with these often sordid individuals, they not only share the prejudices of their more fortunate countrymen, they cherish them in an exaggerated, almost caricatural manner, as though racial or national prejudice were the last bit of 'respectability' they can cling to. It is well known, for instance, that gangsters or yakuza are the most ferocious chauvinists.

Not that the current wave of Asian Gastarbeiter is the first to arrive at Japanese shores. Chinese and Koreans have been arriving in Japan since at least the eighth century, often as highly sophisticated artisans or monks. The circumstances of the last arrival of large numbers of Koreans were not happy; most of them were forced into hard and dangerous jobs by their Japanese colonial masters during the 1930s and 40s. The Iranians, Filipinos, Bangladeshis, and so on, are a new phenomenon, however. Unlike the Chinese and the Koreans, they cannot physically blend into the general population. But like the Koreans and Chinese, many will inevitably produce children with Japanese women or men. Even though a large number will, like Ventura, end up going home, many others will not. So the very least that will happen as a consequence is that the most cherished and tenacious of many Japanese myths is finally destined to disappear; the belief, that is, that Japan, this country bred from Chinese,

Koreans, Mongolians and many indigenous aboriginal tribes, is the last racially homogeneous nation in the world.

IAN BURUMA